Forgotten People

People Without Faces

by
Alejandro Modena

Robert D. Reed Publishers

San Francisco

ii

Copyright © 2001 by Alejandro Modena

All rights reserved

No part of this book may be reproduced without
prior written permission from the publisher or
copyright holder, except for reviewers who may
quote brief passages in a review; nor may any part
of this book be transmitted in any form or by any
means electronic, mechanical, photocopying,
recording or other, without prior written
permission from the publisher or copyright holder.
Permission inquiries should be addressed to Robert
D. Reed Publishers, 720 La Playa, Suite 647, San
Francisco, CA 94121.

ISBN 1-885003-81-1

Library of Congress Catalog Card Number 00-111918

Robert D. Reed Publishers
San Francisco

Contents

Introduction

Dear Reader:

Please allow me to introduce myself. I am a 63-year-old retired businessman. I was born in Israel, raised in Cuba, and now live in California.

You may be wondering why I wrote this book, *Forgotten People: People Without Faces.* Several years ago I had the experience of placing my mother in a convalescent home. I was struck by the isolation of the old people and how little I knew about the rich, though often sad, lives they lead in these homes.

The book begins with the experience of placing a loved one in a home and goes on to describe the humor, the joy and the bitterness of the residents during the last days, weeks, or months of their stay on earth.

My mother, who lived in a convalescent home for a short time before her death, encouraged me to write this book. Then when my wife died, I started writing the book. I spent ten days at my friends' house in Florida—Alan and Sandy Kaplan, and Barbara Pollack, where I wrote the whole book. Then I found an editor, Denise Newman, who guided me on both how to write and sell the book. I was again fortunate when I met Colin Ingram, a writer and editor at Monterey Pacific Publishing, who helped to further develop my book.

When she was in the convalescent home, my mother told me that there is a message that we must tell the world. The message is that by having lived for a long time, the elderly have a vision of the world beyond what the rest of us know of it. By spending time with them we can enrich not only their lives but our own as well.

If you place a loved one in a convalescent home, don't feel guilty. Look for a home that is registered and licensed. Spend some time at the home to see how the staff cares for the residents. Reassure a loved one that he or she needs 24-hour nursing care that is not available anywhere else. Make sure that the residence has continuous care with the same familiar staff, in the same familiar surroundings. The convalescent home should aim to ensure that residents are provided with the best care in a friendly and efficient manner.

It is important that we never forget the people in convalescent homes. You can help by encouraging students to visit convalescent home residents and to create bonds with them. I have seen for myself how much this helps both the residents and the students.

Don't forget a loved one when long term care is a necessity. You never know how much more time an elderly person has left, so make sure that you are doing everything you can for the person you love, and that he or she has the fullest and richest life possible.

That is the basic message of this book. While most of the things I write about actually happened, the names have been changed to protect privacy and some of the events have been altered for the sake of clarity, or to emphasize a point. I hope you enjoy reading it as much as I enjoyed writing it.

1

Anna Goes to the Convalescent Home

Switching roles with our parents is one of the hardest things in life that we have to do. When my wife and I had to take care of her mother, we became parents for the second time. My mother-in-law, Anna, was deteriorating. Her diabetes wasn't under control and we knew sooner or later that she'd need a dialysis machine for her kidneys. On top of this, she'd had several heart attacks. Her health was too precarious for us to take care of her any longer.

I wondered how she had survived this year. It was a miserable year for Anna. She had lost her husband, she had lost her independence by moving in with us, and then she had become sick. My wife, Margaret, told me, "We must look for a convalescent home for Mom."

I didn't know where to start. Anna was included in our search. I asked her to describe what she most wanted in a home. She said, "I don't know, but it better be close so if I need you, you will come to see me." Tears were in her eyes. She knew that this was the end.

Anna was now dressing only in her robe and slippers. She needed help washing herself and dressing. On the other hand, she ate well, she was able to control her sugar intake, and she was able to give herself the necessary insulin shot.

My wife tried to reassure her. "Mom, Alex can have lunch with you, and I will come to see you after work." Anna nodded agreement but her eyes spoke the real truth. She ran her hand over her hair, trying to comb it without a comb. She kept drawing her hand over her hair, combing it without looking at the mirror. She had done it a million times before. She knew exactly where to place her hair.

After deciding on a home, we took Anna there. You looked at her face and you knew that she was thinking about when she had taken her own child, Margaret, to school for the first time many years ago. Margaret had cried and hadn't wanted to stay. But this time Anna's child was taking her to a convalescent home, and she, Anna, didn't want to stay, either.

When Margaret took her mother to the convalescent home, Anna was not combing her hair. They both looked terrible because they both were crying.

▸▸◂▸•O•◂▸◂◂

An orphanage is an institution that cares for homeless children whose parents have died or simply could not care for them. A convalescent home is like an orphanage for old people. The convalescent home can provide services normally unavailable at home like custodial care, therapeutic care and rehabilitative care.

The old people with no one to care for them, or else with a medical condition that requires professional nursing care, end up in a convalescent home. Both the orphans and the convalescents need love and good care. They both need more than food and shelter, however; they need attention and the warmth of human contact.

Anna tried hard to be cheerful about the whole thing. She had been through a lot in her life and had become resilient. She had been born in Russia into a well-to-do family of businessmen. Everything was wonderful until 1917 when the Bolshevik Revolution broke out. Being middle class, they had to flee the country to China. There they found hardship. Overnight their wealth evaporated, and Anna's life went from riches to rags.

At the age of nine, Anna worked in a garment factory, making hats. In China she met her husband. They were married there and in 1944 she gave birth to their daughter, Margaret. In 1948 they decided to leave China and went to Australia where they found more hardship. Finally, in 1952, Anna's dream came true and they were admitted into the United States.

Anna had told us, "I had a good life. Let me be in the convalescent home. I need 24-hour supervision. If I stay in your house you'll become horribly stressed."

She was right, but we still felt that we had ripped her away from her foundations: the house, the neighbors, the grocery store, the beauty parlor, the coffee shops, the laundry and the shops she enjoyed going to with her grandchildren.

Anna had asked us to check out the staff. Are they reliable? Could she count on them?

"You know I'll be depending on them for my survival," she told us, desperately hoping that we were really listening to her. It is very easy to talk, but it is hard to listen.

Cleanliness was also very important to Anna. There should be no institutional smell; most of the convalescent homes smelled like urine or bad institutional cooking.

Anna had asked us to inspect the home thoroughly and to check into state agency reports. Are there any nurses or doctors on the premises? The rooms should be bright and sunny with fresh paint and a clean floor and, on top of all this, the home should be affordable. We told Anna that we would help her pay the expenses.

I asked my wife if we were doing the right thing. I asked her many, many times, what are we doing? Is it so hard to keep Anna with us at home? But we knew if we wanted to keep our sanity we would have to put her in a convalescent home.

>─┤─◆⟩─O─◆┤─┤◄

We found a place near us that met most of our conditions. There were beds for a hundred and fifty residents, although only a hundred people were staying there. The staff was kind and friendly. They weren't standing with their arms folded, chatting; they were helping the residents.

My wife and I took Anna for a visit. She looked so old and hopeless, she hardly was able to get out the car and walk to the home.

"Can I get you a wheelchair?" I asked Anna. I didn't want to embarrass her.

"Yes, Alex, it is a long journey and I want to see everything." Surprisingly, Anna looked very pleased, with a luminous happiness on her face.

I got her a wheelchair and took her inside. Then we were ready for lunch. An elderly man was playing piano in the dining room. There was a pause in the playing, and the man who was playing left the room. I wheeled Anna to the piano. Her now frail fingers touched the keys. She looked up at me with a sad, sweet smile. "You know, I used to be pretty good. Margaret used to play the piano in Australia. When we came to the United States we gave her a choice to play the piano or not. She chose the wrong one. That's why we don't have a piano in our house."

That day they served chicken, rice and carrots for lunch, and we all ate together. For dessert we had chocolate cake and coffee. Anna said in a soft voice so no one would hear, "The food is adequate." She looked contented after filling her stomach.

The main meal at the home was lunch, and dinner was light. They didn't want the residents to go to bed after eating heavy food.

I told Anna, "This was better than home." She looked at me and reassured me that she was going to be all right at the home.

There was a notice on the bulletin board that said: Things to do today: 1) Get up. 2) Survive. 3) Go to bed.

After meeting her roommates, Anna agreed to move in. We only brought a few of her things. If she needed anything we'd bring it to her later. She knew she wasn't going to last long. We brought her portable color television set, her makeup set, toiletry set, night gowns, a robe, underwear, a few dresses and shoes.

When you looked at my mother-in-law you saw an elderly lady, short and not too heavy. She was a brunette with brown eyes, chubby cheeks, glasses and an old-fashioned hairdo, very serious but with a vibrant personality. My wife inherited those traits from her mother.

Anna, only a few months ago, was a woman who enjoyed life, laughing, gossiping, taking excellent care of her appearance, and living in a big house. Now she had to adjust to a room with two roommates. We wondered how she was going to stand it.

The first night we left her in the convalescent home we couldn't sleep. We couldn't wait for morning to see her. We were wondering how she slept. The traffic was heavy next morning. It seemed to me that everybody was traveling to the convalescent home. The traffic lights were so slow-once you miss a light you miss all the lights.

We arrived early and Anna was already washed and ready for breakfast. She greeted us and said with a bit of pride in her voice, "I have an appointment with the beauty parlor to have my hair done, and a manicure and pedicure." She obviously hadn't stopped living; she was using the facilities.

But in spite of that, suddenly Anna was a resident of a convalescent home, one of the forgotten people. My daily visits deepened my respect for and understanding of the residents, listening to their stories, observing their daily routines and becoming a part of their lives.

2

Oscar

The convalescent home where my mother-in-law, Anna, lives is a freshly painted, solid building that covers half a block. Next to it is a rundown apartment building filled with children of all ages. The convalescent home is quiet. The apartment building is noisy. The buildings stand a world apart. The residents of the apartment building never mingle with the people in the convalescent home. You'd think that the children would ride their bikes or play ball in the huge parking lot of the home, but they don't. If a ball falls on the convalescent home's grounds, none of the children will come to get it.

An invisible but powerful line separates the two buildings. A girl will ride her bike in front of her house and suddenly she will stop when she reaches the convalescent home. All the children have been raised since birth to fear the convalescent home. They are poor and they can't afford to lose any of their toys or clothes, but once they leave them on the convalescent home grounds, they are lost.

One day when I was visiting Anna, a skinny Hispanic boy who looked like four or five years old got the courage to walk into the convalescent home. Most likely, somebody had dared him to come in. Being scared but curious, he decided to take the dare. He ran in and out of the automatic doors five or six times. The sixth time I stopped him.

"Let me go," he shouted, and ran off. The next day the Hispanic boy appeared again, wearing shorts two sizes too big for him and a dirty T-shirt with a rip across the back. He was dirty and his knees were full of scabs. Gorgeous, huge brown eyes stared at the old people.

As he entered the home he was mumbling, unsure of himself, but then he looked in my direction and bravely raised his voice: "My name is Oscar. What is your name?" The boy walked toward me. He was impatient. He wanted an answer right away.

"Alex," I answered. I was wondering what a small boy was doing here all alone. I asked him, "How old are you?"

He showed me four fingers. I said, "Four years old."

He said, "No, I am four and a half."

"Why aren't you showing me four and a half fingers?" I asked.

"I can't do it," He said.

I tried by myself and I realized that I couldn't bend my finger very well, either.

"Do you live here, Mister?" Oscar grabbed my hand.

I shook his little hand and I told him "No."

It was three o'clock in the afternoon, the time when the old people got their snacks, and today it was ice cream. The nurse's aide was wheeling a wagon with ice cream. She looked like an ice cream vendor, with white pants, white shirt, white apron, white cap and a bell. The nurse's aide approached Oscar. Oscar froze. He wanted ice-cream but he didn't have any money. He looked inside the wagon and saw several large containers of ice-cream. There was vanilla, strawberry and chocolate. He also saw the bell and he was dying to ring it. He asked the nurse's aide if he could ring the bell. The nurse's aide told him, "Yes, you may ring the bell, but what flavor do you like?".

"Is it free?"

"Yes, it is. Strawberry is good."

"I don't like strawberry."

"What do you like?"

"I only like vanilla," he said looking down. No stranger had ever given him a free ice cream before.

He had seen an ice cream vendor in his neighborhood, but when he begged his mother for money, she'd always said no. He'd watch the other kids eating ice cream and he'd ask them for a lick.

The nurse gave him a vanilla ice cream cone and let him ring the bell. When he finished his cone Oscar said to me, "This is pretty good. I should come here every day. My mother told me this is a home for the old and sick people and I should never come here." Then he looked me over and said, "You aren't old and sick."

"I came to visit someone I love," I said, still wondering what a little boy was doing at the home. I didn't ask him. I went outside to watch Oscar running home to the noisy apartment building.

The people there were loud. Instead of talking to each other, they yelled. You could hear the names of children being called: "Oscar!" "Maria!" etc. The windows were open and you could also hear the stereos, radios and televisions playing loudly. The children and grown ups were all yelling at each other. It was summer. It was hot.

Meanwhile the convalescent home was quiet, even with the televisions on.

3

The Grandchildren

Anna was one of the luckiest residents in the convalescent home. All the residents at the home envied her because she had her family support. We came to see her every day. Very few residents had visitors even though they had families living not too far away from the home. When they were both still in high school, my daughter Sophia, a senior, and my son Benjamin, a freshman, decided to decorate Anna's room in the convalescent home. It was actually Sophia who wanted to make the room cozier. She brought over her stuffed animals and old dolls for Grandma. Anna remembered exactly when Sophia had received each of the stuffed animals. Which one she won at the school fair, which ones were from her birthdays, and which one a special boy had given her. Anna was happy that the grandchildren kept her company and showed interest in her new living arrangements.

"Sophia, are you sure you want to give me those stuffed animals?"

"Yes, Grandma, I outgrew them." She sounded and acted very grown up when she said this.

Anna had always been there for her. She had participated in the whole span of Sophia's life, from her first steps as a baby and, later, to her tap dancing recitals. When Sophia became a cheerleader in high-school, Anna was there at all the football games. There was a special tie between them. They didn't have to talk to each other to know what the other felt.

Anna was living her life through her grandchildren. Every time one of her grandchildren was successful it was thanks to her. She nagged them and told them how lucky they were living in the United States. She, herself, had barely completed primary school in China. At an early age she was working half a day at the hat factory and half a day was going to school.

When they came to the convalescent home Sophia and Ben brought a rainbow bedspread to cover the bed and pillows which they had bought with their own money. They also brought a bulletin board covered with family pictures and hung it in her room. There were happy pictures of the family, vacations, holidays, weddings and letters that Anna had received. It was also Sophia who insisted that Grandma should have a phone. "Grandma can call us any time if she needs us. She can use the speed dial," she argued.

Everything worked just fine; that is, until we got the first phone bill. Margaret and I were ready to scream. We accused the staff before looking closely at the bills, but once we did we could see that it was clearly Sophia who had made all the calls from Anna's room. We gave her two choices: to collect the money from the friends whom she called or to pay the bill herself, which she chose to do. She was working at a local drugstore at the time and it took her a month to pay it off. When she paid it, however, she subtracted the basic monthly charges, as if to say that she wasn't giving in to us completely.

After this had occurred, when Sophia was there, Anna got out of bed with a sad expression on her face. She looked tired, but definitely angry. "Sophia, you made fools of us."

"I'm sorry."

"Please don't do it again."

"Grandma, I promise. I learned my lesson."

"What lesson did you learn, Sophia? Next time not to be caught?" Anna raised her voice and looked straight at Sophia.

Sophia tried to reassure Anna and to win back her trust. She told her, "I didn't know how expensive phone calls were. At home I used the phone and I didn't pay the bill." There were tears in Sophia's eyes as she said this.

"Well, Sophia, I believe you. It is forgiven and forgotten." Anna was smiling when she said this to Sophia.

While Sophia came to the convalescent home once or twice a week, Ben came every day to see his grandmother. He was kind and conscientious to her. His dark hair was always in his eyes, but it only partly concealed the pain he felt for his aging grandmother. He was a lefty. You could notice it right away since he wore his watch on the right wrist.

Since Margaret and I were working and Sophia had a part time job after school, we didn't want Ben to go home to an empty house. He came every day after school to visit his grandmother and to do his homework in her room. Sometimes when I came from work I'd find both of them fast asleep-Anna in her bed and Benjamin in a chair next to her.

Ben met one of the residents, Laura, and thought she could be a good friend to his grandmother. At home, Ben wasn't allowed to watch baseball games during school days, only on the weekend. At the convalescent home he watched the games with his grandmother and Laura.

His grandmother spoiled him, and because she was hungry for his company she let him watch. Laura joined them, since Anna had the best television set at the home. Ben enjoyed Laura's presence since she was able to discuss the game with him; Anna actually didn't care for baseball but enjoyed the company

One day when Ben arrived at the home he stopped at Laura's room. "Are you watching the game?"

"Yes, at my television. Your grandmother doesn't want to watch the game."

"Laura, come and join us," Ben said, and continued on to Anna's room

Anna greeted Ben and asked him, "Did you come to see me or the game? Please don't invite anybody else to watch with us."

"But Grandma, this is an important game and I want Laura to be with us."

Anna was jealous. She didn't want to share him with the other residents so she asked him, "Are you hungry dear? I have an apple for you."

"Thank you, Grandma."

Laura was wheeling her wheelchair to Anna's room and was yelling; "We are winning, eight to three, thanks to the good pitcher."

The game lasted half an hour more and the score was still eight to three. After the game,

Ben left. Laura also left. Anna was complaining because she was all alone. She complained to me that Ben spent too much time with the other residents and left her alone. I told her Ben was special. "Don't nag him," I said, "make him feel welcome."

One day Anna told me, "I remember when Sophia and Benjamin were little. I had a large mirror in the family room and when the little ones put their dirty hand prints on the mirror I didn't have the heart to erase their finger prints from the mirror. After several weeks they faded away. I miss those fingerprints and that mirror."

The Camp

Besides carrying her grandchildren's pictures, Anna carried a few letters in her purse that they had written to her. One of her favorites was written in crayon and decorated with flowers by her granddaughter.

Dear Grandmother.
I am in camp.
Write!
Love, Kisses,
Kisses.
Sophia.

The letters, postcards and birthdays cards that Sophia and Ben had written meant a lot to her. Anna had an enormous box filled with letters, neatly tied with ribbons. She insisted on bringing the box to the home. When she had nothing to do she read the letters over and over again. Those were her sweet memories.

Anna told Sophia, "I was always the middle person between you and your parents. One particular incident stands out in my memory."

"Which one?" Sophia was waiting eagerly for an answer

"Do you remember when you were ten years old and your class went to a YMCA camp to learn about nature?"

"Yes, I was all excited." Sophia had told us, "I was going to have a great time at camp. I was spending a whole week with my friends."

"I remember how you left, with a suitcase of clothes and a backpack with goodies and stuffed animals. Some of the stuffed animals are on my bed."

"Grandma do you want to give Oscar some of the stuffed animals?" Sophia gazed at her grandmother.

"Oh no! Those are just like my children." Anna continued recalling the story. The camp adventure had lasted only five days. The girls had left on Monday and had come back on Friday. It was nice and quiet at home. Ben got all the attention.

On Friday we all went to pick up Sophia. We were excited to see her and hear about her week. When she got off the bus we saw that she was sad and angry. She hugged us and when we got to the car she asked, "Mom, Dad and Grandma, do you love me?"

Margaret and I looked at each other and deferred to Anna as the leader. "Of course we love you," Anna told her.

"Mom, Dad and Grandma, why didn't you write me?"

"Sophia, you left on Monday after breakfast and came back on Friday before lunch. You were only three full days without us," Anna told her.

"Grandma, everybody got letters and packages except me," Sophia told us through her tears. "Mom, Grandma, everybody told me that you don't like me, since you didn't write. I wrote you every day."

We assured her that we hadn't received any of her letters yet.

"I even wrote Ben." She was crying and crying. We couldn't calm her down. It was late afternoon. We took her home. Anna told us, "Let her take a nap; she will feel better once she gets up." But when she awoke she was still crying. She told us, half choking, "Everybody was teasing me, telling me that you aren't my parents, and you don't like me."

We didn't know how to calm her down. We started talking with her. We asked her what might make her feel better. "I don't want to go to school Monday because they'll mock me again."

We asked her who, and what exactly they told her.

"Leslie and Jennifer told me that you adopted me."

She looked so sad; her eyes were full with tears. It looked like somebody over-filled a glass and any moment it would begin to pour out.

"Leslie and Jennifer picked me as their roommate," Sophia said. "Leslie told me, 'Sophia, I got a large package filled with candies and comic books from my mom and dad.' 'So did I,' Jennifer said, 'I got a package and a latter from my mom.'

"I told them 'I'll probably get a package or a letter tomorrow.' But nothing came for me. The third day Jennifer asked me, 'Were you adopted, Sophia?'

'No,' I said, 'I don't think so.'

'Why aren't you getting any letters from your parents?'

'I don't know.'

"Mom, Dad and Grandma, everybody in the camp got packages and letters, except the twins. Jennifer said that's because they were adopted. It didn't take long 'til everyone in the camp spread rumors that I was adopted. That's why I don't want to go to school."

We told Sophia it was okay with us, since she was an A student. Then Anna took out her baby book and showed her the birth certificate and her baby pictures. That still wasn't enough to convince Sophia. Anna told her, "If you weren't my grandchild would I knit you a sweater and bake you cookies?"

Sophia abruptly changed the subject. "Mom, Grandma, I have nothing to wear."

"The closet is full of clothes. Did you look in your closet, granddaughter?" Anna asked her sweetly.

"Grandma! They are old clothes and out of style."

We finally ended the talking. Sophia was a hard bargainer. We took her to an amusement park and then bought her a new outfit.

Grandma went with us to buy the new outfit. Sophia also got a stuffed animal to match the outfit. Later, Anna defended us by telling Sophia, "Your parents followed the directions they got in the letter before you went to camp. They got a list of things for you to take to camp, but they weren't informed that they should write you letters." Finally, Sophia forgave us.

Then Anna said, "Sophia, those are supposedly your friends. But I wish you would cross them off your list. They mocked you. They are having a good time on your account."

Years later, when the subject of a new outfit came up again, Anna taught Sophia the value of money. When Sophia was about twelve years old, she approached Anna and asked if she would buy her a new outfit. She had to have it. Anna told her that she didn't have any money, but added, "Sophia you can earn it by stuffing envelopes." Sophia worked very hard to earn her money. When she finally reached her goal, Anna took her to the store to buy the outfit. Sophia tried on the outfit, but when she realized that she had to pay for it with the money she had earned, she changed her mind.

Anna told her, "It's different, isn't it, when you have to work for it?"

"Grandma, how did you know that I wouldn't buy the outfit?"

"Because, Sophia, you are becoming older and wiser."

Parents learn from camp, too. When Ben went to camp we were prepared. Anna reminded us to write letters for Ben weeks before he left for camp. While he was there we mailed the letters to him and sent him packages. When he got the packages the cookies were stale but the kids ate them anyway and were happy.

The Treasure

In a European family the oldest member is the leader, and any question that arises is answered by the leader. Anna was the oldest member of our family. As long as she lived she was our chief and leader. We all went to her for advice. Sophia honored her by letting her be the first one to sign her school yearbook. Anna could hardly write, but she wrote "Good luck, love, Anna." Following her, I signed the book in blue pen and Margaret in red ink. Later on Sophia took the yearbook to be signed by her friends.

One Sunday afternoon we came to visit Anna at the home. Margaret, Anna and I were drinking hot tea and the children had coke. Margaret also brought us a tray of cheese, crackers and grapes. We were telling stories and remembering a particular event.

In the same year that Sophia went to camp, she decided she need-ed a higher allowance and asked her mother. Margaret took the easy road and told her to ask Dad. I told her to ask Grandma. Anna told her,

"You will have to earn it." Sophia was ten years old at the time.

Besides cleaning her room and getting good grades, Sophia had to make lunches for the family. Every day she made four bag lunches. Each bag got a peanut butter sandwich, a juice, a fruit and a treat. Sometimes she wrote us notes. She wrote her brother, inviting him to have lunch with her and her friends.

"Ben, do you remember having fun eating lunch with the older kids?" Anna asked him.

"I was in heaven eating lunch with Sophia's friends."

Sophia wrote Margaret and me lunch notes that she loved us. One day she gave me two lunch bags.

"I can only eat one lunch. Why two bags?"

"Promise me that you only open the bags at lunch time." I promised, kissed her and left for work. At lunch time I opened the bags. One bag had a baloney sandwich, potato chips, orange juice and cookies. The second bag consisted of junk. There was a broken necklace, a few stickers, broken crayons and plastic animals. I looked at it quickly, then threw it in the garbage.

When I arrived home my daughter waited for me, which she normally never did. She was usually in her room listening to records or talking on the phone to her friends.

"Where's my bag?"

"Oh, the one you gave me?"

"Dad, did you bring it back?"

"Sophia, I thought you gave it to me to keep it."

"No, father, I only lent it to you."

"Sophia, you gave your father two lunch bags?" Anna asked.

"Yes, Grandma."

"Sophia, what was in the second bag?"

"Grandma, those things in the bag were my treasures. I wanted Dad to see how beautiful my necklace was that I wore at Ben's birthday party, and stickers that the teacher gave me when I did a good job, and plastic animals you gave to me."

Sophia was devastated. I felt terrible since I had thrown it in the garbage. I started to talk about it with her, to see if she would forgive me. I knew in my heart I had lost her trust. It took months to regain her confidence, and that was only because of Anna. Anna told her to test me again by giving me other treasures to see if I would bring them back. I learned my lesson. If a child gives you something you must take care of it.

Back at the convalescent home we were nibbling the cheese and sipping our cups of tea. Ben finished his coke and was still thirsty.

Margaret asked him, "Ben, do you want a cup of tea?"

"No, Ma. I'm not sick."

"Ben, you can have some cold water."

"Thank you, Ma, I don't want anything. Let Sophia tell us her story."

It was Sophia's turn and she told us her side of the story. "I remember that evening we went to the office looking for my treasures. We reached the garbage can and to our surprise it was empty. The janitor had already cleaned the room and dumped it in the dumpster."

Sophia was diddling on a scrap of paper, trying to draw the necklace, the plastic animals, the whole treasure that she had lost. I looked at her now as an adult and remembered when she was a small child. I had not played her game. I had been in a hurry for her to grow, but I should have stopped the clock and enjoyed her little game..

Why are we always in such a rush for our children to grow up? When they are one, we can't wait for them to be two. When they are in first grade, we can't wait for them to be in second. Why can't we just enjoy our children at the age they are instead of wishing they are something else?

"Sophia," I told her, "I was very, very sad, when I learned you wanted your things back."

"Me too, Dad. I almost cried, but I held my tears back. I told you it was okay, that it was my fault since I hadn't told you to bring it back." Sophia looked at me, still sad, years after the incident.

She rushed over to me and hugged me, burying her head in my neck, and now she was crying. "Dad, you took me to a toy store and wanted me to replace my treasures. I told you that you didn't have to do it." Then she added, "I remember that I made you a good lunch that day. It had all the ingredients for a healthy lunch and also I packed a napkin in the lunch bag."

Anna said, "Sophia it is very hard to be a parent and to always do the right thing.

By this time, Ben was excited. He wanted to tell us his side of the story. Anna and I told him, "Go ahead."

"I remember that Dad didn't bring Sophia's toys home, and he told us, 'I hope the janitor didn't get rid of the treasure' Dad took us to the office and we found the original treasure plus more toys."

"Ben, that was a beautiful story, and I love you very much for it. Dad, I know that it is very hard to be a parent.," Sophia said. Sophia looked at me, smiling, and told me, "Dad, I forgive you." I smiled back, and then a little chuckle came out of her. And in a moment, we were looking at each other, laughing out loud. The mirth was so infectious that Anna, Margaret and Ben had to join in. When the laughter finally subsided, there was a different feeling in the room-a nice feeling.

It had taken ten years, but now it was forgiven

It was getting late. Anna was visibly slumping. She told us, "I really enjoyed the company and the stories. I'm tired now, but I hope to see you tomorrow."

We knew then, that Anna had enjoyed her time with us at the convalescent home and, in turn, we were happy to have spent those precious hours with her.

4

The Bad Girl

Oscar came to see the old people every day. As he approached the convalescent home he'd see them waiting, sitting by the window. They were sitting in their wheelchairs pushing each other in order to get a better view of the street, anticipating his arrival. Even though John was eighty-five years old and a secret alcoholic, he was healthy enough to wheel his wheelchair faster because he wanted the best view. He was a real bully. He sniffed at the other residents and then laughed when he got the best seat. When he didn't he whined. Bill, a retired school teacher, was a gentleman until he entered the race. Then he became a disrespectful person like John. Being cooped up all day up in their rooms, they wanted to see the outside world. They didn't respect each other and honor the first one to have the best place. Instead, they pushed each other and the bully always won. They shouted, cried or yelled at each other. They swore at each other. The loser waited for the winner to leave the place so he could enjoy it.

Every day was the same confrontation. The staff gave up. They knew that sooner or later the older people would work the problems out on their own.

I don't know if Oscar realized how much he meant to them. He did become very attached to one of the women whose name was Laura. Laura could hardly gobble her breakfast food fast enough. She was in a hurry to race her wheelchair to the glass window. She wanted to be the first one to greet Oscar.

Laura was a unique woman. Although she had Parkinson's disease, she was very poised and graceful; she could have been an aristocrat the way she carried herself. She had curly white hair and her skin was also very white. Even though she was over eighty years old she had very few wrinkles. But when she took her dentures out she suddenly looked a hundred years old.

Laura was one of the few residents who didn't need eye glasses or a hearing aid. She loved Oscar and she was always telling him stories. When Oscar arrived that afternoon, Laura told him this story.

"She was only ten years old. She was so bad that the teachers didn't know what to do with her. They punished her, but it didn't do any good. Her parents punished her but still she was bad. When other children were standing in line she pushed them and they fell. When the teacher asked all the children to be quiet she started yelling. At lunch she took the other kids' lunches. Her father and mother spanked her, but still she was bad.

"Finally, feeling there was nothing else to do, her father decided to take her out into the ocean and leave her there. They rowed far out and then he threw her from the boat. The little girl screamed for help but her father rowed to shore, keeping his back to her.

"The girl started to swim to land. On her way she saw ferocious sharks, an octopus and other big fish. The sharks thought they'd eat her, but when they found out that she was the bad girl, they swam away. None of the fish wanted anything to do with her. They didn't even want to eat such a bad girl.

"The bad girl realized that nobody, not even the sharks, wanted to have anything to do with her. Finally, after many hours of swimming, the little girl reached land and ran home. Through her tears she told her father and mother that she wouldn't be bad anymore. From that experience she learned her lesson and became good."

Oscar's eyes were wide open. He had been listening closely the whole time. Laura asked him what had he learned from this story. Oscar replied that we should always be good.

It was three o'clock in the afternoon and time for a snack, Ovaltine and cookies. Oscar grabbed some cookies and a drink. He filled his mouth with cookies and Ovaltine. He shoveled one cookie after another into his mouth. He wasn't chewing the cookies—only filling his mouth. Then, suddenly, he vomited it all out and ran away.

The floor was a mess.

I thought about the story Laura had told. It didn't make any sense. How come if you are bad a shark won't eat you, but if you are good they will eat you? Is the moral of the story that it is better to be bad than good? I asked Oscar and he explained it to me. The moral of the story is that nobody, not even a fierce shark, wants to be with a bad person. Seeing this, the girl learned her lesson and became good. If a five-year-old kid could get the concept, I guess I should have been able to get it, too.

After he had spit out the contents of his mouth. Oscar had left the home in a hurry. The residents followed him with their eyes. A few minutes later I saw him sitting on the sidewalk, hitting himself. He slapped his hand hard. He hit his knee, and punched himself. All the time I heard him saying, "...a bad boy, bad boy." He hit himself again. Then I heard him saying;, "I should have cleaned the mess I made."

I approached him and asked, "Why did you run away?"

"Alex, you know why."

"Why?"

"I vomited and I didn't clean the floor or ask someone to clean it." He started to cry. "They will never let me to come to see them again, because I am bad."

I looked at Oscar and gave him a tissue paper so he could dry his tears. "Oscar, you aren't a bad boy, only a kid, and kids sometimes make mistakes."

"When I spilled my milk at home, my mother hit me and told me that I am a bad boy."

"Oscar, you aren't bad, only a little mischievous."

"I don't know why she got mad at me. It is my milk. I can do whatever I want with it."

I told Oscar, "No, your mother loves you very much and doesn't want you to waste food."

I assured Oscar that if he felt better, he could come back and have another glass of Ovaltine and cookies-and maybe eat slower this time.

Oscar didn't want to come back just then. He told me, "I'll come tomorrow. Good-bye, Alex."

I went back to the convalescent home and I saw that the residents were sitting close to each other. Oscar, their one diversion, was gone. Now they were talking to each other again, laughing over secret things. That was how they spent their days.

5

Oscar's New Clothes

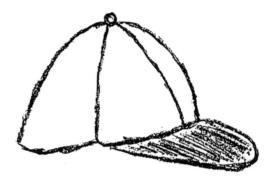

Oscar was a four-and-a-half year old Hispanic boy. He was small for his age, and skinny. He was very active and could never sit still. He spoke Spanish at home and English on the street. Oscar always dressed in ragged clothes. He had a yellow and orange T-shirt two sizes too big for him; brown pants, a torn khaki jacket with a zipper that didn't work, and sandals. In contrast, he had large, gorgeous brown eyes that were opened as wide as saucers. His black hair looked like tar and his smile reminded me of an angel.

Anna, my mother-in-law who was in the convalescent home, couldn't stand the way Oscar was dressed. It reminded her of the way her mother had had to dress her when she was a child in China. At the age of nine Anna had worked in a garment factory making hats. Her family was very poor. She only worked in the morning, for half a day. In the afternoon she went to school. The winter was very cold. Anna was always cold because she was dressed poorly and fed poorly. She remembered that her mother had hit her when she outgrew and tore her old coat. She told her mother that the coat was all worn out. Seven kids had worn it before Anna. Sometimes it was so cold she had to wear several outfits in order to keep warm.

At school, Anna met some girls who worked at the doll factory. Being a little girl, she wished she worked at the doll factory instead at the hat factory, but she was lucky that her mother had gotten her any job.

Anna was smart, and she traded a fur hat for a doll. She called her doll "Sunshine," and every place she went, she took her doll.

That was 53 years ago. Now, remembering her own childhood deprivation, she told my wife and me that we should shop for some clothes for Oscar, so we took him to the local department store.

When we got there, Oscar slowly walked into the store. His feet were weak and wobbly. The bright lights startled his eyes. Oscar looked at us. His face was white and his little hand, damp, cold and trembling, grabbed my hand. This boy who normally spoke at a speed of sixty miles an hour in either English or Spanish, suddenly became silent.

All Oscar's clothes had been given to his parents second-hand by friends, or were from Goodwill. This was his first time in a department store. He had never owned any new clothes.

Oscar looked around and was afraid to move. He held Margaret's and my hand as we went up to the children's department on the second floor. He was afraid of the escalator and so we had to go up and down with him. The second time he became more sure of himself and started running up and down the escalator. That was fun. He loved the free rides. The tenth time we finally stopped him.

"Enough, we came here to buy clothes," I said.

Oscar's life was just like an escalator—up and down. Sometimes there wasn't any food at home, only beer. His mother made sure that there was always beer in the refrigerator. His father was a gardener who worked very hard in the hot sun and demanded beer after work.

One time Oscar asked me, "Do you like beer?"

"Yes, I do. When I drink beer, I relax."

"I drunk beer, I hate it. I was hungry and that was the only food we had."

"Did you get sick?"

"Yes, but now we have food and I don't have to drink beer any more."

In the department store, Oscar was almost peeing in his pants, and he let us know it by pinching the front of his pants. We had to find a bathroom in a hurry. Here was also a new experience; he had never seen a urinal before. Luckily, he was able to reach it, and this made him happy. But he couldn't reach the sink; I had to lift and help him wash his hands.

After the bathroom, Oscar was running around the store and throwing stuffed animals. He told me they felt soft and good. What a sight this child was. He needed to be scrubbed and bathed for a week. His hair was in knots and his fingernails long and dirt filled. But bad appearance or no, it was time to try on some clothes.

He whined, "Do I have to?"

"Yes, you do. If you want clothes that fit you, you have to try them on," I told him.

"I never tried any clothes at Goodwill," he said.

His mother had bought him the cheapest clothes at the store, without much concern about fit. He also never had any new toys. We looked at a wall filled with peg toys. Hundreds of pegs with die-cast cars hanging from them. There were army cars, racing cars, jeeps, modern and antique cars. Oscar asked me if I would buy him a die-cast car, then looked at the car with begging eyes. We told him that he could pick one out. He was so happy, and thanked and kissed both of us.

I looked at his selection and asked, "Oscar, why did you pick out the Volkswagen bug?"

"Because that's what my father drives."

"Oscar would you like to have another car? Maybe a big truck or a pick-up?"

"Why?"

"Because we can get two cars almost as cheaply as one."

"No, thank you. My father has only one car and that's what I want."

After that, we bought him T-shirts, two pairs of shorts, Levis, a sweater, underwear, a baseball cap, tennis shoes and socks. The whole bill was less than a hundred dollars. Oscar loved the cap the best. It had an emblem of the local baseball team on it. He asked me if the team was the champion. I told him if he wore the T-shirts and cap he'd help them win the games and maybe become the champion.

That afternoon I brought Oscar to the convalescent home to show Anna the goodies. Once again it was three o'clock and time for a snack, just like every day. The snack was ice cream and the nurse's aid didn't have to ask Oscar what flavor he wanted; she gave him a vanilla. Anna asked for some. I told her no. She said, "Don't be so mean," but I was only thinking about her diabetes.

Anna asked Oscar, "Do you like the new clothes?"

Oscar let out a sigh and said, "Thank you, thank you, thank you."

Anna noticed Oscar holding something in his hand very tightly.

"What do you have in your hand, Oscar?"

"Would you like to see it, Anna? It's a white car and I love it." Oscar showed her the car.

"It is a beautiful car, take good care of it."

Oscar left without the clothes. I had to catch him. The only thing he had taken was the little white car. I gave him the clothes and told him I expected him to wear them. Once again Oscar let out a sigh and said, "Thank you, thank you, thank you."

After he had gone I turned to Anna. "Do you think Oscar will wear the clothes? I don't think he likes them," I said.

Anna looked at me and said, "Oscar is young. Young boys like toys better than clothes. Oscar is a very normal boy."

Anna was happy she had suggested buying the clothes. She had been a poor child in a foreign country, just like Oscar. Nobody had ever done anything like that for her.

Anna kissed Margaret and me, and we went home. On the way home I told my wife, "Wasn't it a lovely day, spending time with Oscar?"

Margaret replied, "I know we made Anna happy. About Oscar, we'll have to wait and see."

6

Grandparents

Everybody needs grandparents. Laura, Anna and Bill informally adopted Oscar. Laura was the best grandmother.

After having lunch with my mother-in-law, Anna, in her room, I noticed that I still had time before I went to work. I lay back in my chair and quickly fell asleep. I must have only been sleeping a few minutes when Oscar touched my shoulder. He stood by me in his rags. I wondered why he hadn't changed into his new clothes. A few weeks had passed since we had bought him the clothes and he had only worn his new baseball cap. He asked me if our baseball team was winning. I told him no, since he wasn't wearing the new T-shirt. When I asked him what he had done with the clothes, he shyly said he had hidden them under his bed. He looked at Anna, expecting sympathy, but Anna gave him a dirty look.

"When are you going to wear the new clothes?" I asked.

"I don't know," he answered.

Laura came in and joined the conversation. "Don't you want to look nice, Oscar? You are a handsome looking boy. Change your clothes and come back."

Oscar didn't answer, and walked away. He knew he was in trouble.

Laura asked me, "Do you think that Oscar will come back or is this the last time we are going to see him?

"He will be back. You want to bet that he will be back?"

Laura said, "I don't have any money, but I don't mind betting you."

"If you win I will take you to lunch at a local restaurant."

Meanwhile, Oscar had gone home and had changed his clothes. When he came back he was accompanied by a young Hispanic woman. Oscar was wearing a light blue T-shirt, navy blue shorts and tennis shoes. His mother had washed his face and combed his hair. He had brought his mother with him to thank us for the clothes. Everybody was happy to see Oscar back.

Oscar's mother was small, dark and skinny. Her black hair was long and her gorgeous, huge brown eyes looked just like Oscar's. Her name was Dora. Oscar told me he was afraid to tell his mother that he was coming here, because she had told him this is the home for the old and sick people and that he shouldn't bother them.

Laura, who spoke Spanish, assured Oscar's mother that he behaved well here and that he was better off here than playing in the street, and that his visits were a high point of their day.

Dora was very timid. She didn't want to cause any problems. She knew that her four-and-a-half-year-old boy was full of energy and could cause a lot of problems. Oscar was a very active boy and could get on your nerves.

The convalescent home was now part of Oscar's territory and he didn't want to be sent far away from home to a new babysitter-if he was bad his next door neighbor wouldn't be able to take care of him. So Oscar decided to show his mother how good he was.

Dora asked Laura, "Is Oscar good?" and Laura translated.

Anna told Dora, "I have two grandchildren and Oscar behaves better. Look at him sitting so quietly."

Bill looked at Oscar and wondered how long this act would last. He told Oscar's mother, "El niño se porta muy bien."

Seeing Oscar with his new clothes reminded Laura of a story to tell us. A few of the residents listened. Dora was still there and Oscar sat still on his mother's lap. She was surprised by how glued to her he was. He didn't move, which was even stranger to her. She embraced him, hugging him tightly, enjoying his company.

Normally, Dora had little time for Oscar. She was a cleaning lady and she had to help her husband earn the rent money. She didn't have any family here. Oscar had never met his own grandparents; he was raised only by his parents. Now Dora smiled broadly and said, "El es muy guapo."

This time Bill translated for the others, "He is very handsome."

Laura's Story

Laura began telling a story to the other residents, pausing occasionally to translate for Dora.

"Once upon a time there was a grandmother who loved her grandson very much. She traveled all over the world, and every time she came home she brought the little boy toys and clothes but she never spent any time with him. Once the grandson asked her to play with him.

"'I don't have any time to play with you,' she said, 'I must go and get you more toys and clothes.'

"The boy's room was full of clothes and toys, but he didn't have anybody to play with him. The grandmother returned with more toys and clothes, but she still didn't have time to play. Now he had even more toys but no one to play with. He had many clothes, but no one to show them off to.

"Again his grandmother left and came back with more toys and clothes. Now the house was crammed full of toys and clothes. The little boy again asked his grandmother to play with him. Again she said 'I don't have any time. I must go get you more toys and clothes.'

"The little boy was very sad. He said. 'I wish I had a grandmother that didn't bring me toys and clothes, but played with me.'"

Laura told the residents that the grandmother should have stopped buying and started playing with her grandchild. She said that a child needs a father and a mother to raise him. He also needs two sets of grandparents. The grandparents will give him clothes, toys and make time to play with him. Through the child, the grandparents revive their youth. The parents will discipline the child and the grandparents will spoil him. Oscar didn't have any real grandparents. So Anna, Laura and Bill informally adopted him.

Laura asked Oscar if he liked the story.

"I did like the story," Oscar said, "But I wish I had a grandmother that gave me clothes, toys, and who played with me."

Anna said, "I gave you clothes."

Oscar replied, "I know."

Anna said, "Why didn't you wear them?"

Oscar said, "I was afraid to show them to my mother. I thought that she would blame me for stealing them. But, see, I am wearing them now."

Anna replied, "Oscar you are a very handsome boy in your new clothes."

Then Laura said to Oscar, "I am the grandmother who played with you."

Oscar was smiling. He ran over and hugged Laura, and he said to his mother, "Ella es mi abuela." (She is my grandmother.)

Laura said, "Yes, I am your grandmother, Oscar, and Bill is your grandfather."

And Bill said, "I gave you toys, Oscar, just like a real grandfather."

⤐┉⟐┉⤏

It was time for Dora to leave. Laura assured her that she could leave Oscar at the home. "Señora, Oscar is a good boy, and he is safe here. Please leave him with us."

"Are you sure? If he is bad send him home."

"Okay," Laura replied, looking at Oscar.

Oscar's mother told Oscar, "Hijo, portate bien!" (Son, be good!)

Oscar couldn't wait to see his mother leave. Then he asked me, "Is it time for a snack?"

"You have to wait a few more moments."

Oscar was frisky, he couldn't sit still. He sat on the chair with his legs crossed. Then he got off the chair and sat under the chair with his legs crossed. Then he heard an ice cream vendor's truck outside. "Are we getting ice cream for a snack today?"

I told him, "No, we have run out of ice cream." They were serving Jell-O. Oscar had never had Jell-O. The nurse's aide asked him, "What flavor do you like?"

"What do you have?"

"We have lime, strawberry and orange."

Oscar took the orange Jell-O. He started to eat it, but it started to jump around. He wasn't able to catch it with a spoon. Bill told him to grab the Jell-O in his hand, but it was so slippery that Oscar had a hard time grabbing it.

Bill said, "Hold it with three of your fingers and cut it into small parts."

Oscar followed the instruction. For the first time in his life he ate Jell-O. Anna scolded him and said, "Don't dirty your new clothes, be careful, Oscar."

Laura just giggled and enjoyed the sight. She asked Oscar, "Do you like it?"

"It is okay but I wish I had ice cream."

Oscar finished eating his Jell-O and left without saying good-bye. But at least he had learned a few things. In addition to being introduced to Jell-O, Oscar knew that grandparents should take time to play with grandchildren, and that clothes and toys are not enough.

Just as important, the residents felt for a few minutes that they were being good grandparents.

7

Bill, the P.E. Teacher

Bill was the youngest resident in the convalescent home. At seventy years old, he had had several heart attacks, but otherwise he was in good shape. He had been a fourth grade teacher. He said he had never gotten attached to any of his students. By the end of the year he "flushed them down," so he would be ready for the next school year. If he worried about his previous class he wouldn't be able to do a good job with the new students. He gave 100% of himself during the school year.

Bill's full name was William Young Thomas, but he signed his name Bill Y.T. and had earned the nickname of "Bill Yours Truly." When he retired he became a substitute teacher-for the money and the company of the students and the teachers, since at that time he lived alone.

After thirty-seven years of marriage his wife, a "fluff ball" (a woman that doesn't want to do any work) left him for a younger man. They didn't have any children, so he was quite alone. He needed 24-hour supervision because of frequent episodes of chest pain requiring medication. That forced him to go to the convalescent home.

After his very active career, the loneliness was unbearable for Bill. Lying in bed seeing the same scenery made him feel useless, and so he wandered out to the railroad tracks and stood there, hoping to get hit by a train. This happened twice, and twice the police brought him back to the convalescent home before he was injured.

Luckily, the supervisor discovered Bill's talent for consulting and teaching. He gave him an office. That was Bill's reason to get up every morning. He got dressed in a suit and tie. Bill was slim and tall, with large blue eyes and a full head of snow white hair. He looked rumpled like he always did. Even with a fresh shirt on, part of the shirt tail was always sticking out of his belt.

Otherwise he looked like a movie star. Bill put a sign on the door, "Creative World," and he became the center of creative activity at the home. He took Polaroid pictures of every resident in the home, pasted them on different-colored construction paper and hung them on the wall like a mural. Under each picture was a label with the name of the resident, plus one word describing them. He labeled himself "Hercules." Anna was "Housewife." Laura was "Gutsy." Laura's two roommates, Mary and Ruth, were "Happy" and "Generous."

One day when several of the residents were gathered together, Bill began to tell them about one of his experiences substituting in a local high school.

He was teaching geometry and the students had a handout to work through. He noticed that instead of doing their math problems, two girls were discussing what to write to the P.E. teacher to be excused from the class. After crumpling up several attempts and throwing them in the wastebasket, they finally got the perfect letter. It read:

Dear Miss So and So:
Please excuse my daughter from P.E. She just turned sixteen years old and we got her diamond earrings. We are afraid that if she participates in P.E. exercises she will lose the earrings and if she leaves them in her locker somebody will steal them..
Yours, (the mother's name).

The one who wrote the letter asked her friend to forge her mother's signature. They left the class proud, mission accomplished. They didn't realize that someone might suspect a forgery. During that class, Bill had known what the girls were doing. The following week he met one of the girls and asked how her excuse had worked with the P.E. teacher. The girl told him she had gotten in trouble with both teacher and her parents. Now she had to do double P.E. for a month—regular class and after school.

After telling his story, Bill organized some of the residents for an exercise class. He gave a set of weights to my mother-in-law and she told him, "I must be crazy," and dropped the weights. But Laura, who was in worse condition than Anna, grabbed the weights and asked if she could keep them. This was the beginning of a serious exercise program. Ruth loved the program. She was always positive and cheerful. Mary participated by chewing on the weights—she was in a different world.

Later that day, when Oscar was there, he approached Bill and asked him, "Mister, can you teach me how to use the weights?"

"Oscar, you always call me Bill. What's this "mister" business?"

"I thought if I am polite and call you 'mister,' you will teach me how to use the weights."

"Oscar, you are too young," Bill said. But when he looked at Oscar's pleading puppy eyes, he couldn't refuse. "Okay, Oscar, you can lead the class."

They did twenty minutes of exercises. Everybody was tired and happy. Oscar told Laura; "My weights are blue because I am a boy. Yours are pink because you are a girl."

Laura laughed. It was time to go to the next activity. Oscar had been so interested in the exercise class he left without a snack.

Bill told me, "Healthy body, healthy mind. That is my motto."

Bill insisted that everybody do their daily exercises. Bill told the residents, "If you had done your exercises when you were young, maybe you wouldn't have landed in the convalescent home. But if you want to live longer, you should exercise."

Instead of staring at the empty walls like zombies, several of the residents started to do exercises, lifting weights and pushing their wheelchairs. After a week of exercising, Mary seemed happier, Ruth even more generous, Laura still gutsy, and Bill, himself, just a bit more Hercules.

8

The Lazy Boy

Oscar approached the brown leather reclining chair near where Laura was sitting and asked her what kind of a chair it was. "It's a Lazy Boy," she said. Oscar was happy since it wasn't a lazy girl chair. He sat on it and felt like a king. Mary, who had Alzheimer's disease, approached Oscar and rudely pushed him from the chair. Oscar fell and hit his head, got up and ran, crying. The Lazy Boy was Mary's domain. Nobody messed around with Mary. Mary was a tall, pale, elderly woman. She had hazel eyes, a small face and small mouth, and she looked very mean.

Mary had her daily routine which could not be negotiated. She got up by herself, dressed by herself, and also ate by herself, which was a great help to the nurse's aide at the convalescent home. Next she sat in her Lazy Boy, and this was the way she spent her days.

The following day Oscar said to Mary, "This is a Lazy Boy chair and I should sit in here because I'm a boy." Mary didn't understand him. When he approached her, she roared at him or ground her teeth. Oscar was disturbing her daily routine! Laura, who had Parkinson's disease and was sitting in a wheel chair, told Mary to share the chair with Oscar, and to be nice to him.

Oscar was really mad. He didn't want to share the chair with Mary. He tried to push Mary out of the chair. After all this was a Lazy Boy chair, and not a lazy girl chair. Laura tried to explain it to him that this was only a name brand. The manufacture just gave it this name, but Oscar didn't understand.

Mary actually didn't have any idea where she was; all she knew was that in the morning she woke up, got dressed in one of the many-colored outfits that she had: bright blue, bright red, green, pink or yellow. Mary dressed by herself, went to the bathroom, and went to eat breakfast almost like a robot. Every day she sat in the same chair in the dining room with the same ladies. She sat with Laura, Ruth and Dolores.

Dolores had a daughter who came to see her often. Dolores always complained to her daughter that the food was intolerable, and her daughter brought her some food from home each time she came. Laura noticed that Dolores licked her fingers at mealtime and seemed to be enjoying the convalescent home's food. Laura asked her why she was complaining about the food. Dolores replied, "That's the only way I can bring my daughter to visit me."

Mary ate hot cereals, and never changed her menu. After breakfast the nurse's aide tried to wash her but she never cooperated. She'd just run from the dining room to the living room to sit in her Lazy Boy. In the living room was an upholstered, brown leather sofa, a few rocking chairs and the Lazy Boy. The Lazy Boy chair was upholstered with brown leather that matched the sofa but was torn and patched. Mary didn't remember much, but she remembered that the Lazy Boy was hers.

Laura told Oscar and Mary, "Why don't both of you share the chair?"

Oscar replied, "Good idea."

Mary said, "No."

"Oscar, why don't you sit on Mary's lap?"

Oscar smiled and said, "It's okay with me."

Laura asked, "Mary, is that okay with you?"

"Yes."

And in fact it was more than okay. Mary held Oscar and tried to kiss him. Oscar enjoyed the warm body of an old woman as she held and kissed him. Oscar let her kiss him on the head. Mary had no quarrel with Oscar. It's just that the Lazy Boy was hers, and no one—no one—was going to change that.

9

Bill, the Teacher

OSCAR

Several years ago on a Monday it was raining like cats and dogs. You couldn't see a cloud in the sky because the sky was so dark. It was raining and raining, so hard you could hear the water slapping on the ground. None of the residents had the will to get out of bed. They were snug in their warm beds. Why should they get up? When the weather was ugly, they felt ugly and sad.

Bill, the youngest resident in the convalescent home, was the only one up. He was dressed and looked rumpled like he always did. Not only was part of his shirt sticking out of his pants, this morning the waist of his pants was crooked as though held up by only one side of his suspenders. His pants were gray, his shirt was blue and his tie was red.

Bill had a job to do. He tried to get some of the residents out of bed to do their daily routines, like brushing teeth, washing, going to the bathroom, dressing, eating breakfast and going on to daily activities

That morning I got a phone call at my office to come over and see Anna, my mother-in-law. She had refused to get out of bed, and they wanted me to do something. While I was there, Oscar arrived. He seemed to know when the worst time to show up was. He was soaking wet and despite all the work with the residents, we had to tend to Oscar. Bill dried and dressed him in a huge T-shirt. By this time, most of the residents had grudgingly gotten out of bed. When that was done, and morning ablutions finished, Bill gathered all of us and told another story about his teaching experiences.

He had been substituting in one of the local high schools. Bill told us that he didn't trust any of his students to check the attendance. He remembered one day when he was teaching and one of the students had asked him if she could check the attendance of the class. He told her to go ahead, but wondered why she had wanted to do it. When she returned the attendance sheet there were twenty students marked present on the attendance sheet while there were twenty-five students in the class. She had marked five as absent. He asked her, "Why did you mark five absent?" She replied, "I don't like those kids and I hope they will get in trouble." Since then he didn't trust any students to do the attendance sheet.

"The moment I laid my eyes on Sabrina I knew this was trouble," Bill told us. "Sabrina was a fifteen-year-old blond girl. "When I walked to the classroom, Sabrina was there, wiggling her butt and asking me if I was her substitute teacher. She was chewing bubble gum and blowing bubbles and popping them. I told her that chewing gum isn't allowed in the classroom.

"Sabrina asked if she could be my assistant, like with erasing the blackboard, checking the attendance and other duties. When I told her no, she got mad and told me that I was in big trouble. I asked her to get rid of the gum. So she gave away five whole packages—seventy-five sticks—of gum to her classmates. Then she casually walked all around the classroom, blowing and popping bubbles. The rest of the class followed her, all twenty-five of them. They all paraded around the classroom, chewing gum and popping bubbles.

"I was supposed to teach social studies that day, but nothing got taught. It doesn't matter how long you have been teaching, you should always be prepared for anything. I was caught off guard."

It was still raining. Oscar asked us if we were allowed to chew gum in the convalescent home. I told him that only cows chew and he isn't a cow. Then it was lunch time. I told Oscar that after lunch Bill was going to tell us another story.

During lunch I heard the residents of the convalescent home discussing Bill's story about Sabrina and the bubble gum. Laura said, "What wrong with our youth? Laura, the resident with Parkinson's disease, wore lipstick every day, but had trouble applying it. It was too high on one side of her mouth and too low on the other, giving her a peculiar, lop-sided expression.

In contrast, Ruth was immaculate. The chairs in the room were arranged in neat rows, as in a theater. If a resident dared to move a chair, as soon as the seat was vacant Ruth would move it back into its formal place.

Ruth replied, "Our youth don't have respect for the older people."

Bill said, "The most important commandment is 'Honor your father and your mother.'"

Laura said, "I wish we had more young people coming to visit us."

Then Bill asked, "Did we come to visit senior citizens at convalescent homes when we were younger?"

Ruth said, "No, but we had to make a living."

Laura, with her lop-sided expression, said, "I hope that we teach our grandchildren how important the older generation is."

You know," Bill said, "in Japan they honor the elderly people. They have a holiday called, 'Respect for the Aged Day.' It is on September 15th. The children, as part of their curriculum in school, visit convalescent homes. The young people spend the day with the old people. They make them a party."

Laura said, "Here we have Father's Day and Mother's day and then we forget our parents the rest of the year."

Then lunch was over.

A Free Meal

After lunch, once our bellies were full and everyone was relaxed, Bill told us about another incident that had happened to him. "One day I went to a barbecue restaurant called 'Chicken, Chicken.' I ordered my meal and when I went to pay for it, the manager came out, called me by my name, and said that the meal was on them. I wondered how he knew my name, since this was the first time that I had walked into this establishment. He asked me if I knew the bus-boy, Jamie. I told him yes, I knew Jamie. I had substituted in his school and I'd had him five or six times in Math. Jamie came out and took my tray to one of the tables where I sat down. I asked him if he had paid for my meal. He told me no. He had asked his boss to give me a free meal, since I was his best teacher. I told him if he thought that I would change his grade in math because of a free meal he had the wrong teacher. But I had embarrassed him. His face turned red and he said, 'No, no, you did something no other teacher has ever done for me, and I'm grateful.'

"Jamie had been in this country for six months. He'd come from Guatemala and was eager to learn English and other subjects. He was in pre-algebra and he hated that class. He called it 'dummy math.' I noticed that he, as well as some other students, didn't belong in that class, but none of them could speak English very well. I asked the principal and the counselor to test them and let them go to the next algebra class.

"The vocabulary needed for algebra is very limited. I took the few words they needed to know and translated them into Spanish. Later, Jamie informed me that he was in the regular algebra class and was getting As. He was beaming. His face was lighting up. I felt like a million dollars and," Bill told us with a big smile, "I had been able to do something for this young man."

Oscar listened to the story and told Bill "When I go to kindergarten I want you to be my teacher." Bill got excited and asked Oscar if he wanted to learn how to write his name. But surprisingly, Oscar didn't want to. He said he had arthritis in his right hand. Oscar didn't know such basic things as the names of colors, but he knew the names of the diseases at the convalescent home, like Parkinson's, diabetes and Alzheimer's.

Meanwhile the rain had stopped, Oscar's clothes were dry and it was time for him to go home. Bill was disappointed at not being able to teach Oscar how to write his name. When Oscar left the convalescent home Bill decided to follow him, staying well back so he wouldn't be noticed. Oscar saw a group of kids playing ball and went over to join them. Some of the other kids teased him because he was smaller. Oscar felt hurt and he left the group.

He sat on the sidewalk, watching the other kids playing. Bill watched him for a while, and realized that Oscar was very timid and he was afraid of failing. Then Bill knew why Oscar had not wanted to learn how to write his name. It was a test, and the way Oscar had sought to avoid being tested was to lie and say that he had arthritis.

Bill told himself, "Be patient. When Oscar is ready he will approach me."

Several weeks passed and one day Oscar did ask Bill to teach him how to write his name. Bill was very happy to do this. He already had prepared a piece of white cardboard on which he wrote in red "OSCAR." He asked Oscar to trace his name. Oscar repeated the letters of his name: "O" written like a circle, "S" like a snake, "C" is half a circle, "A" is three sticks, and "R" a is a circle and two sticks.

It didn't take long for Oscar to learn how to write his name. He had forgotten the excuse he had used with Bill. Oscar started writing his name. He wrote his name on any scrap of paper he could find. He even wrote his name several times on the wall with crayon. But Bill didn't scold him, he just took a sponge and soap and started cleaning the wall. Oscar noticed what he was doing and told Bill, "I am sorry." He also started cleaning the wall. Both of them were working hard, scrubbing the wall. The informal grandfather and his informally-adopted grandson were sharing the same task—and they seemed to be enjoying it.

10

The Man with Two Faces

Every morning Ruth greeted the other residents of the home. She wore a blue dress and a scarf, with flowers and matching shoes. You could hardly see the wrinkles on her face. She told the residents how good they looked, even if they looked sick and worn out. When she told Laura how good she looked, Laura replied, "You can see me and I can see you, so I guess we are both alive and well." As long as Ruth continued to compliment the residents the morale of the home remained relatively high. She demanded that each resident tell her that they were okay. She asked Mary, "Are you okay?" Mary didn't answer. "Well?" she asked again.

Finally Mary said, "I'm okay."

Most of the able residents loved to play bingo. Oscar loved to distribute the bingo cards. Laura, Betty, Anna, Ruth, Bill, Mary and John enjoyed the game. The prizes were candies. Oscar always cheered for

Laura because she was the only one who shared her winnings with him.

"I got you the best card," Oscar whispered to her. There was a little jealousy among the residents over Oscar's attention to Laura. Bill asked Oscar how his arthritis was. Oscar said it was fine, since he learned to write his name. He pulled the numbers and showed them to Laura first because he didn't know how to read them.

Bingo is a very simple game. It consists of bingo cards, bingo balls, and a person or a machine that selects the balls. You only have to know how to read the numbers and letters which are on the bingo cards and on the bingo balls. Any player whose card shows the drawn number covers the appropriate spot on the card. The first player to completely cover a horizontal, vertical or diagonal row of numbers wins. Then that player must call out "bingo."

When Ruth won she told everyone she had won because she looked great and felt great, and that's what it takes to win. Laura won a few games, but Ruth won most of them. Everybody won some games. Anna was the most unlucky. She was ready to cry. Nobody noticed this except Ruth, who had a heart of gold. She decided to cheat and let Anna win the last game when the winner took all the leftover candies.

I was worried that Anna would eat all the candies, because of her diabetes, but at that moment she had no interest in candy-she just wanted to be a winner and not a loser.

Afterwards, Ruth asked all the players if they enjoyed playing bingo. She demanded an answer from each one.

Betty told her, "It was fun."

Laura still had had trouble with her lipstick; she looked at the others with her usual lopsided expression. "Now I have something to give to Oscar," she said. She had won five candies and gave Oscar four. She ate the chocolate covered marshmallow, letting it melt in her mouth. She wished she had more of those candies; the others were hard and she didn't like to suck on them.

Anna told how she used to play mah-jong once a week with three other ladies. Each week they alternated houses. They started to play at 10 a.m. and kept going until 4 p.m. The hostess would serve lunch. Anna missed those days. Ruth asked if her daughter knew how to play mah-jong. Anna said, "No, not now, but I gave her a game set. It was my mother's. When my mother died I learned to play mah-jong. When I die, my daughter will learn to play mah-jong."

Then Ruth asked John if he had enjoyed the bingo game. He grudgingly admitted that he had.

John was eighty-five years old and a secret alcoholic. He was a bright person but the alcohol had almost killed him. After paying his bills, whatever money was left he spent on alcohol. He had to drink in order to function, and always looked like he had just rolled out of bed. His shirt was too short for him and his pants were torn. One suspender had slid off his shoulder and he wore raggedy slippers. But the most striking thing about John was his face. One side was a nice, friendly, normal face, and the other side had a large, awful-looking scar. Oscar was frightened by John's appearance, but, as it often happens with small children, Oscar was also fascinated by John's scarred face and stayed close to him. John, on the other hand, had little patience or interest in Oscar. After being pestered by Oscar for several minutes, John thought he could get rid of him by telling him a story.

The story began like this. "A long, long time ago in our city there was a man with two faces. How frightening he was. He had Bell's Palsy, which is a bug that destroys half of your face. One side of his face was nice and smooth, and the other side was a frightening sight. So he covered the ugly side of his face with long hair. One day he was walking on the street when he met a beggar. The beggar saw only the nice face and asked him for help. He gave the beggar a strange coin that looked valuable, and the beggar was able to exchange it for some real money. With the money he bought some fishing gear and started fishing. He was very successful and caught lots of fish, which he sold for more money. In a short time he bought a boat. Every day he went fishing and came back with large catches. Almost overnight the poor beggar had become a rich man.

"Meanwhile, the man with the two faces had become poor. One day he approached the former beggar and asked him for help. This time the beggar saw only the ugly side of his face, and he kicked him and told him to go away. Now very angry, the man with the two faces cursed him.

"The next day the former beggar went fishing. There was a storm and he lost his boat. When he reached land nothing seemed to go right anymore, and he became poor again. He remembered the two men, one with the happy face and one with the ugly face. He thought, 'If only I had treated the ugly man well, maybe I wouldn't have become poor again.'"

After the story ended, Oscar looked thoughtful but didn't say anything. Neither did John. He was crunching and chewing the candies he had won at bingo. Oscar imitated him and loosened a baby tooth. John offered to fix it for him. He put a thread in Oscar's mouth, yanked on the thread, and out came the baby tooth. It hurt Oscar and he ran home crying. John kept the tooth. He was planning to reward Oscar but

Oscar didn't come to the home for several days after that.

Everybody missed him. John felt guilty since he had hurt Oscar. He had a quarter to give to Oscar for the tooth.

Laura offered, "Oscar will be back at the next bingo game." But Oscar didn't show up. Oscar was just like a weed that you get used to. He was always moving and noisy. He was alive, and that's what the old people needed.

A few days later I saw Oscar on the street and I approached him. "Oscar, why aren't you coming to the home?"

Oscar put his right hand in front of his mouth and whispered to me, "I lotht my front teeth and I don't want to be called an old man."

I asked him, "Did you lose all four teeth?"

"Yeth, I did."

"How did you lose them?"

"I don't know, but everybody when you are young looth hith teeth. Thath why we call them baby teeth."

I said, "Remember the story about the man with two faces? How the beggar was mean to him and then he became poor?"

Oscar said he remembered.

"Well, then, everybody should be very careful not to call you mean names." I assured Oscar that nobody at the home would call him an old man, and we walked in together.

It was three o'clock in the afternoon, the time when the old people got their snacks, and today it was a vanilla ice cream sandwich. Oscar was happy as long he got ice cream. The nurse's aide who pushed in the ice cream cart was of over-ample proportions. She learned forward over the edge of the upper tray as she pushed, her bosom occasionally dipping into the vanilla, chocolate and strawberry, creating a vivid pattern across her uniform that rivaled the best of modern art.

Oscar saw this and laughed, displaying his missing teeth for all to see. My son, Ben, who was there visiting his grandma, was standing nearby. He took one look at Oscar and said, "Oscar, you look like an old man."

I felt terrible, and looked at Oscar to see his reaction. But he was too happy with the ice cream to be hurt. But between licks he said to Ben, "You better watch out, 'cause now you're going to be poor."

To this day, Ben doesn't know what he meant.

11

Rita and Mike: A True Love

On one of our Sunday visits to Anna at the convalescent home, my wife, Margaret, asked me if I wanted to hear some gossip. Of cause I did. I was ready for gossip. "Did you notice the older couple holding hands?" she said. "They aren't even married and yet he comes every day to see her."

I suggested they were holding hands because they aren't married. My wife asked me if, at their age, we'd be holding hands. "We are married for life and if holding hands makes you happy, then I'm ready to hold hands and to hear the gossip."

Anna told me the names of the older couple: Rita and Mike. Rita's room is next door to Anna's room. Rita was beautiful even at her late age. She was a bleached blond, slim, and her appearance was very important to her. She spent hours on her appearance each day. She was very methodical. She brushed her hair very slowly. Every stroke was a big effort for her since she had arthritis. Then she painted her eyebrows black because she had shaved them off. Finally she put a red lipstick on her lips—the hottest red. Then she put powder on her face. She looked outstanding, just like a royal queen.

Rita completely ignored the other residents. She had been married and divorced four times and had had several affairs. Her four daughters and five stepsons all have different fathers. All together there are twenty grandchildren.

With so many ex-husbands, children and grandchildren, I expected the nursing home to be filled with Rita's relatives, but she only had one steady visitor—her ex-husband, Mike, husband number four.

Mike was a barber in one of the large hotels in the neighborhood. He owned his own barbershop and from its income had saved some money, which he decided to spend in Las Vegas, where he thought he'd be able to find a rich wife. When he arrived there, Mike rented a suite in one of the hotels on the strip. He rented expensive clothes and jewelry, and prepared himself to catch a wealthy wife. He wore a diamond ring, bracelet and a necklace to match.

Rita was a hard working secretary. She had also saved some money over several years, and she had a similar plan to go to Las Vegas to find a rich husband. Rita also rented a suite, coincidentally in the same hotel as Mike, and even more coincidentally, her suite was next to his.

Mike and Rita both had the appearance of millionaires. When they met in the casino, Rita played her role to the hilt. She deserved an Oscar and so did Mike. Rita's suite was filled with roses that Mike sent to her. He took her to dinners and to expensive shows. They gambled and had a good time. After just a few days they got married. Mike was happy because he thought he'd gotten himself a rich wife. Rita was happy because she thought she'd gotten herself a wealthy husband.

Toward the end of their stay in Las Vegas, Rita remarked that since he was so wealthy, he surely wouldn't mind paying her hotel bill. Mike replied that he was going to ask her the same thing. Then Rita asked him directly if he was or wasn't a rich man. He told her that he was a barber. Then he asked her if she was wealthy. She told him she was only a secretary. They both realized that they had been fooled, and they annulled the marriage.

After this adventure, Rita declared bankruptcy and Mike took out a loan to pay off his Las Vegas debt. Many years later, Mike still comes to see Rita every day, and they still laugh about their adventure.

Mike was still healthy and lived in a house and drove a car. Rita was sick and had landed in the convalescent home. Each time he came, Mike was dressed in a red jacket, tie and black slacks; and every time he came, Rita laughed. I asked her, "Why are you laughing at Mike's appearance?" That was when both Mike and Rita told me their story.

Once Rita had settled down in the convalescent home, Mike decided to take her to dinner and to the opera.. He'd had a massage, a haircut, manicure and pedicure, and was dressed to kill. He wore his red wool jacket with black wool slacks, black tie and black patent leather shoes. His black hair was so shiny it reflected some of the red from his jacket.

Red, white and black looked good on him. Red jacket, white shirt, black slacks; a tall slim man that most women would go for. Rita, a blond, wore a red dress and black shoes to match the handsome man's outfit. After dinner Mike walked to the opera house with Rita. On the way he wasn't looking where he was going and stepped in a pile of dog doo. He tried to clean his shoes, but he wasn't very successful, and the smell was very noticeable.

There was nothing else to do but continue walking to the opera house. Mike took Rita to her seat and sat next to her. As it happened, all the ushers were dressed in red jackets, white shirts, ties, black slacks and black shoes. Mike looked just like an usher. Even with his strong smell, people kept asking him to take them to their seats. He refused, and when the manager overheard him, he scolded him and demanded he start working to earn his free seat. When Mike showed him his purchased ticket, the manager apologized. That was why Mike and Rita laughed when Mike wore his usher outfit.

While there was laughter between them over the usher episode and the Las Vegas trip, and a host of other stories, there was also love. It made everyone at the convalescent home feel good to see them— including me.

12

Betty Goes Shopping

Once you stay somewhere for a few months or years you get to
know a place, just like you know your own body. No one can ever
really tell you all about yourself, only you know what you think and
feel.

Betty was Anna's roommate. Betty was a heavy-set woman, a nasty
woman. To others, it seemed like she didn't have a heart, but once you
got to know her, it was clear that her toughness was only a defense.
Her eyes were big and hazel. She couldn't find clothes in her large size,
so she had to wear men's clothes. Her cheeks were red and sunken
where she'd lost her teeth. The rest of her teeth were gray since she
didn't take good care of them. All in all, Betty had an unattractive,
almost vulgar appearance.

She had only one child, a daughter, who looked like a young version of her mother and who lived just few blocks from the home.
Betty had raised her daughter all on her own. She had given the
daughter everything she had desired but, despite this, Betty believed

that her daughter felt that her mother hadn't done enough for her.

Betty remembered how she had treated her daughter on a particular holiday. When the family had gathered together for dinner and her daughter, at the age of seven, had broken a plate and was ready to cry, Betty told everybody to drop their plates and break them-and they all did! Everybody was laughing; they didn't want to hurt the child's feelings.

Betty had always bought her daughter the most popular toys in town. She had wanted to make her daughter happy. But now, during the year that Betty was living in the convalescent home, her daughter came by only a few times. Once she dropped off a book and told Betty to read it, and when she finished, her daughter would come back and quiz her. But her daughter hadn't shown up.

One day I happened to see the daughter in the street, and asked when she might be coming to see her mother. She answered, "When my heart tells me, and so far my heart hasn't."

Mother's Day was coming. Betty was looking at the Mother's Day ads in the newspapers. One read "The perfect gift for mom is only from this department store." Another read, "Give Mom something so special it could only come from xxxxx store!" Still others said "On sale! Our entire stock of women's dresses, shoes, purses, sweaters, pajamas, etc., is 40% off the marked price." Betty was hoping that her daughter would come to see her with a present on Mother's Day. Her daughter never showed up. Instead she had gone to Las Vegas.

Betty felt so bad. Her heart was hurting. It felt like she had been stabbed. She told everybody, "Who cares about Mother's Day? My daughter loves me and every day is Mother's Day." Then Betty ran crying into her room and, for want of anything better to do, she started to read the book her daughter had brought her.

Betty thought about her daughter all day long as she went about her daily activities, walking around, eating, taking a bath, reading, and sometimes even thinking about her in her dreams.

Betty never quit thinking about her.

One day Oscar arrived for his afternoon visit and, after staring at her book for a long time, he asked Betty what she was reading. Betty was nasty to him. "I don't have time to talk to you. I must finish reading this book. Any moment my daughter will come and quiz me about the damn book."

Oscar nagged Betty to tell him the story of the book, and finally she conceded. Oscar crawled onto her lap. "Once upon a time there were two brothers who wanted a bicycle, but their father could only afford to buy one bike. He took the children to the store. The children chose the bike. He told them that they must visit the store every day, and the one who continued visiting the store the longest time would get the bike.

Every day after school the boys went to the store to see the bike. The store owner let the children ride it and polish it. One day one of the boys told his brother that going to watch the bike was stupid and he wasn't going to go anymore. But the other boy continued visiting the bike every day for another week, riding it, polishing and loving it. At the end of the week the owner of the store gave the bike to the boy who had stayed. He told him his father had already paid for the bike and had told him to give it to the one with the most perseverance." Betty told Oscar, "We've learned from this story that if you want a reward you must work for it."

Betty continued reading the book and waiting for her daughter, but her daughter never showed up. Oscar couldn't understand why she hadn't come. He told Betty that he would come to see her, and that she should start a new book. Oscar insisted that Betty should go to Bill's room, the "Creative Room," where there were many books-good fat ones.

Oscar showed Betty that he could write his name, and Betty showed him how to write her name. Then Oscar decided to learn to write everybody's name in the home.

When Betty had moved from her apartment house to the convalescent home, she had stored all her furniture in a storage compartment. What was great about this storage facility was that it was a closed concrete building with different compartments, or lockers. It was always secure and dry. The manager was an old guy from Brooklyn, friendly and always helping customers store their treasures.

He'd said, "Gee, Lady, ya got sum really nice stuff here. Too bad ya gotta pay so much to store it each month, when your money could go to better things."

She had paid rent faithfully, until she, too, realized that she was throwing her money away. Betty knew that she was not getting younger and she would never leave the convalescent home. One day she called the storage manager and asked him if he could sell her goods. She told him, "I will pay you for your work."

"Sure lady. For you I'd do it for nuttin'."

With the money that she got, Betty decided to buy a Mother's Day present for each resident of the convalescent home. Betty asked one of the nurse's aides to take her to the local department store. It was only five blocks away. The nurse's aide wheeled Betty to the department store and on their way they passed Betty's daughter's house. Betty tried to control herself. She didn't want to visit the house even though it had a lovely garden in front of the house, a lawn, rose bushes and seasonal flowers. Her daughter spent all her free time taking care of the garden.

Of course, Betty really wanted to see her daughter. Maybe her daughter would reassure her that she was doing the right thing in buying all the presents. She asked the nurse's aide to ring the doorbell. The nurse's aide rang the doorbell and rang again in case Betty's daughter didn't hear her. At first Betty thought her daughter was hiding from her, so she asked the nurse's aide to look around the house, to peek in the windows and see if her daughter was really away. Then Betty got out of the wheelchair and went by herself to the front door and pressed the buzzer. She rang it for a long time but nobody answered. Betty noticed that her daughter's car was not parked in front of the house, and she realized her daughter was working away from home—it was only 10 o'clock in the morning.

Betty was angry and sad at the same time. She knew her daughter was away, and she also knew her daughter wasn't coming to see her. The nurse's aide asked her, "What would you say to your daughter if you saw her now?"

"I would ask her to join me, to help buy the presents for the residents, and maybe I would buy her an outfit," Betty said crying. The nurse's aide had a napkin and dried Betty's tears.

Once they entered the department store, Betty bought two outfits for herself. She was a strikingly large, heavy woman. She looked almost like a giant. Her hair was gray and long, and loosely braided into a ponytail. Betty hadn't taken good care of herself since her daughter had left her. She had lost interest in living.

But now Betty bought a green sweat suit from the men's department, to wear for exercising. She also bought a pink dress that she would wear just in case her daughter might come to visit her. She bought it at the "pretty and plump" department. She was the only customer there.

Both the nurse's aide and the saleslady assisted her. They were very helpful. Then she concentrated on the gifts for the residents and staff. She bought scarves, towels and coffee cups labeled with names of the staff and residents. She was really happy doing a good deed.

For Anna, her roommate, who was very delicate, she bought a silk scarf. For Mary, whose memory was not so good, she bought a blanket that she could fold and touch. For Bill and John she bought coffee mugs filled with candies, with their names on the mugs. For Laura she bought a yellow sweater. Betty said to the nurse's aide,

"Laura told me that she is always cold because she has thin blood."

Her last thought was Oscar. What to get for the sweet little boy who gave her so much pleasure with his visits. She thought and thought and looked and looked. Finally, she saw the biggest truck in the whole store, red with big black wheels and a red siren. The staff at the store wrapped the presents and, back at the home, Betty distributed them to the residents. The residents were very happy.

It was like Christmas in May when Betty gave Oscar the truck. Oscar didn't know what to say—he was speechless. He knew that he couldn't bring it home, so he asked Betty, "Can I keep it here?"

Betty replied, "Yes, Oscar, you can keep it here."

Oscar kissed the truck and ran away without saying a thank you or a good-bye.

But that didn't spoil Betty's good mood. She felt happier than she had in a long time. And still her daughter didn't come.

13

Bill's Story

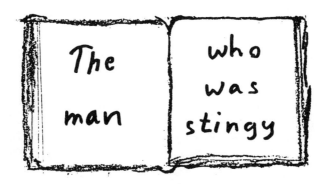

Sunday was a special day for our family. In the morning we went to church and then we went to watch the children as they played soccer, basketball, or baseball. Then we went to lunch and a movie. Then things changed after my mother-in-law, Anna, was in the convalescent home. Every Sunday after the children's sports, we came to visit Anna. There was always a priest or a minister or a rabbi who held a Sunday service. After the service the fortunate residents were left with their visitors and the rest, most of them, with just their memories.

There was always something good to eat. We had fruits, cakes, cookies, coffee and tea. The home received donations of leftover wedding cakes and sweets from bar mitzvahs or bat mitzvahs. Some of the cakes were damaged and instead of throwing them away some local bakeries gave them to the convalescent home. The cakes looked pitiful or forgotten, just like the forgotten people.

On Sunday afternoon, Bill would treat us to one of his stories. We stuffed ourselves with goodies and we listened to Bill's charming stories about his teaching experiences. One Sunday, Bill began like this.

"I was substituting in one of the local high schools, and I noticed that one of my students wasn't doing his work. I only had five students and it was easy to spot him. His name was Robert, and he was short, overweight and wore baggy clothes. He bleached his hair and wore it short.

"Robert wasn't an active kid. He didn't play any sports. He was lost in the shuffle and I knew he had been promoted because of his age, not by how much he had learned. Most of the teachers forgot about him, as long as he didn't cause any problems.

"On the day I was substituting, Robert was supposed to read a book and answer the questions at the back of the book.

I asked him:, 'Why aren't you doing your work?'

He replied, 'Have you read this book?'

'No,' I answered, 'I haven't read the book.'

He mimicked me saying, in a cynical tone of voice, 'I didn't read the book.'

I gave him an angry look and said, 'What did you say?'

'Why aren't you reading the book, so you can explain it to us?' Robert boy said.

"I paused for a moment and thought that maybe he was right, so later I borrowed a copy of the book from of the library and I spent the weekend reading it. On Monday, still substituting for that same class, I informed Robert that I had read the book. He then told me that he was glad I had read the book because I could now do his assignment for him. Realizing that he was making a fool of me, I got mad and I told him that he was supposed to read the book and I expected a book report. After that he stopped talking back, and the following week he read the book and gave me a book report.

"Robert told me that I was the first teacher who paid him attention and didn't treat him as a forgotten person."

That ended Bill's story but Laura asked Bill to tell us another story. "Bill, tell us what the book was about that you read that weekend."

Bill didn't respond, so Ruth added, "Don't tease us, Bill. Please tell us about the book."

Bill couldn't resist a bit more teasing, and he asked the residents, "Are you sure you want to hear about the book today, or should I tell it to you tomorrow?" They all wanted to hear the story today, so Bill began to tell the story of the book.

"Once upon a time there was an old man who was very stingy. His name was Raymond and he was married for the third time to a woman named Linda. Raymond was very wealthy, and they lived in a palace—a real palace, not an imitation one. There was an iron gate and nobody could enter without Raymond's permission. If anyone tried to get in without Raymond turning off the electricity, they would be shocked. He loved to see people get shocks, like the cleaning lady or the mailman.

Raymond had a very big ego. He used the pronoun "I" whenever he made decisions in order to focus on himself; he had the power and he enjoyed belittling other people."

Laura asked, "How did he become so wealthy?"

Bill answered, "I will tell you. As a young man he was poor but was ambitious. He decided to become a plastic surgeon. He didn't have any money and his parents couldn't afford to send him to school. He joined the army and they paid for his schooling. After the army he went into private practice and made lots of money. Any time he had any extra money he invested it in real estate."

Ruth said, "I did the same thing. I bought buildings and that's how I made my fortune."

Laura looked at Ruth and said sarcastically, "Look where you ended up—in the same convalescent home as me!"

Ruth was very diplomatic. She didn't want to cause any problems, so she said, "Let Bill continue telling the story."

Bill said, "Raymond didn't trust anybody and he loved conflict and turmoil. He was loud and he blamed other people for his own mistakes. He never made an attempt to tame his ego. Raymond used words and phrases such as 'absolutely,' 'certainly' and 'I know I can.' He was a self-made man. When he looked into a mirror it seemed to say, 'I love myself, and I value myself, and that is all that I care about.'

"Raymond kept a journal, and anyone that offended him was entered. He carried grudges. One day when he went to a restaurant with a group of people and they asked him to share the bill, he insisted on a separate bill because he had eaten less and he didn't want to pay for the other people's food. 'My bill is this much,' he protested, 'Why should I pay more?'

'But,' they said, 'in the past, sometimes we paid for your bill.'

'I am not going to take care of freeloaders,' Raymond shouted. 'You people are trying to take advantage of me. You are low class scum. I don't give charity.'

"By then the argument had aroused the interest of the entire restaurant and Raymond had his way when the manager made peace to save his facility further embarrassment.

"As nasty as he was, Raymond still sought happiness, as we all do. But happiness eluded him. He believed that the world ought to be as he was rather than as it is.

"Gradually, Raymond lost all his friends. He stayed at home with his wife and he counted his money. He had one room in the palace that was full of money. The wall paper of this room was actually made of money bills. Every day at sunrise he ran to the room and stared at the walls and ceiling.

"One morning he asked his wife, 'Did anybody call us?'

'No, Raymond,' she said, 'but may I call my mother?'

'No, Linda,' he said, 'that costs money. I cannot afford it. Remember, I was poor once. Now I am rich, but I could become poor again.'

"His wife was dying to leave him, but she was afraid. She had never had a job and was scared she couldn't make a living. Sometimes she snuck out of the house and spent some of his money, but she always had to come back and face his terrible rage.

"Raymond spent from sunrise to sundown watching his money. He not only enjoyed looking at it, but if he watched his money all the time, he wouldn't use electricity watching TV or listening to the radio.

"The money made him happy. There was a gleam in his eyes when he handled his money. He was not only stingy with his wife and everyone else, he was also stingy with himself. He wore old clothes that were torn and dirty. One day he lost his belt so he wore a rope instead. He told his wife, 'Am I not a genius to wear a rope instead of a belt?'

His wife told him, "Please don't wear a torn sweater when you go outside."

He replied, 'If I go to the store with torn clothes, they will still take my money, won't they?'"

Gradually, Raymond grew old and senile. He hid himself in his favorite room, the money room. He spent days there, just staring at the money. No one saw much of him, including his wife. After a while she simply forgot about him. Finally, he died, old and wrinkled. No one mourned his passing; in fact, he was dead for quite a while before anyone was even aware of it."

Bill finished telling the story. Laura was frightened, and asked Bill, "What will happen to me if I lose my money and I cannot pay to live here anymore?"

"Don't worry, Laura," Bill replied, "you donated your house and they will take care of you for the rest of your life."

Laura said, "I was poor, then I made money, and now I am poor again."

Ruth said, "I understand the story. Be nice to people, and if you are rich, be generous and everybody will remember you. If you are stingy and mean, everybody will forget you."

By this time, everyone was tired. The residents went to their rooms to prepare for dinner. We left before dinner, exhausted from an afternoon of storytelling with the forgotten people. I told my wife, "Raymond got what he deserved, but not Laura, Bill, Ruth and Betty. They shouldn't be forgotten."

14

Ruth's Family

It was Ruth's 86th birthday, and her whole family had been invited to attend a party at the convalescent home. Ruth was tiny with short legs and a chunky body, a big head and long black hair that partially covered her face. She was near-sighted and wore thick glasses. Some of her hair stood straight up on the top of her head just like a Scottish Terrier. She had several deep wrinkles on her face but her hands had remained soft and smooth.

Ruth had two married sons and two grandchildren. Her elder son was blessed with two kids, a boy and a girl, and he brought them to the birthday party. His wife didn't want to come; she claimed the place smelled like urine and it made her sick. Although he came this time, this son had often used the children as an excuse not to visit Ruth. Her younger son, with no children, also showed up very infrequently. But for this occasion he and his wife had come.

There was not exactly a festive mood at the party. Ruth was crying and no one knew what to do about it. That is, except Oscar. He asked her why she was crying. "Do your tears taste good?" he naively asked. She told him they tasted salty. Tears came easily to Ruth. All she had to do was feel sad. Now tears were running down her face and her nose was dripping. She didn't make a sound but you knew she was crying.

The more her sons and Oscar talked to her, the more the tears came dripping down. Oscar tried to cheer her up by acting silly. He made faces and stuck out his tongue and made silly gestures. Then he tried to tickle her. He told her he had to do it for her because she wouldn't laugh if she tickled herself. That's what Bill had taught him. When Oscar was sad, Bill had told him to tickle himself. Oscar tried but it didn't help, so Bill had tickled him and they had laughed for hours. So Oscar tried this with Ruth but had no success.

Her elder son brought Ruth a piece of chocolate nut cake and she stopped crying in order to eat it. It was Ruth's favorite kind of cake, and this one was particularly moist and delicious.

Ruth was wearing a navy blue dress with a silver belt. The buttons were silver to match the belt. The dress was too long for her. No one had taken the time to shorten it. She wore black patent leather shoes without stockings, because she couldn't get the stockings on by herself. One of the nurses had combed her hair and put a flower in it. After all, she was the birthday girl. Ruth had also put some make-up and rouge and lipstick on.

Everybody wished her a happy birthday. Oscar and the grandchildren sang the Happy Birthday song. Ruth asked her granddaughter, who was in the seventh grade, if she liked school and if she got good grades. She said, "I get good grades because my father rewards me with money. But I don't like school—only recess and lunch." Ruth told her that she would make an excellent recreation director.

"Why?" she asked.

"Because you are a social butterfly. That means you get along well with everyone."

Ruth thought that by complimenting her granddaughter, she would come more often to see her, but she was mistaken. Her granddaughter wanted to go home already. She'd had cake and ice cream and had filled her stomach.

Ruth's grandson, who was younger and was in the fifth grade, hadn't said a word to his grandmother the whole time. When he finally got pushed near to her, he was dragging his feet. When his mom and dad were ready to leave, Ruth asked him when he was coming back. He didn't answer.

Ruth's elder son didn't like to come to the convalescent home because he didn't like to see her aging. When he did come, he only stayed half an hour, and it was torture for him. He couldn't stand seeing his mother cry. This visit, by the time she had stopped crying he was about to leave, but by then Ruth was ready to talk. She looked at him with great love and concern. Was he eating well? Did he get enough sleep? Was his wife nice to him? Did he dress well? Was he happy with his children? Was he progressing well in his career?

Sometimes the elder son brought his wife and children but they were in such a hurry it was like a hurricane. He had to bribe them to come with him. They, too, didn't like seeing Ruth in such an aged condition.

Her younger son told her, "Mom, you are getting older and fatter since the last time I saw you. You should go on a diet."

"Son, I had to call you to remind you about my birthday and ask you to come for old time's sake," Ruth told him. "I have nothing else to do here but eat. No one ever comes to see me—not you or your brother."

But in spite of their differences, birthdays mean food and presents. Ruth's sons had brought her a TV set. But Ruth wasn't happy. She told them she didn't like to watch TV; she would rather talk to her friends. "I don't think TV will make me a better person," she said, "and the programs use bad language and aren't nice. The news depresses me and the commercials want me to buy things I can't afford and don't need." The biggest present her family could give her, Ruth said, would be coming to see her more often. She wanted to tell her grandchildren the history of the family and all about their relatives that they had never met. But by then Ruth was tired and starting to doze. The sons and their families used this as an excuse to sneak away.

Oscar and I helped clean the room. I was surprised that none of Ruth's family helped clean up. Who did they expect to do it? They ate, drank, used napkins and paper plates and threw them all over the place, while all it would take would be to throw the paper plates, cups and napkins in the wastebasket.

I felt that the family had abandoned both good manners and her. It was the same old story; when we are old and sick nobody wants to be with us. The Eskimos have a solution; they let the old people die in the snow; we let them die in the convalescent home.

The next day Laura, Ruth's roommate, approached her and said, "It was a lovely party." Ruth agreed with her.

"The food was excellent, the cake was great, and the decorations were out of this world." Laura said. "You got a beautiful television. It is better than Anna's, that witch!"

Ruth said, "You think so?"

"Yes, Ruth. Now that you have such a beautiful television I don't have to leave our room and go to Anna's room."

"Do you think Anna will come to watch television with us?"

"Who cares?" Laura turned on the television. It was loud and they were happy. In spite of Ruth's complaining to her sons that she didn't want the TV, she was now proud of it.

Then the cleaning lady started to clean the room. She vacuumed the floor. She went under the beds. She picked up the candy wrappers which lay on the floor. She tried to dust the TV. Ruth watched her like a hawk. She was afraid that she would scratch the new TV. Usually, the residents leave the room so the cleaning ladies can clean the room, but not this time. Ruth was afraid to leave her most valuable possession, the TV.

The new TV had remote control. It was easy for Ruth to control it from her bed. And gradually the TV began to take the place of her sons' visits.

Mary Jane

Sometimes what you see may deceive you; the human mind travels much farther than the human body. Ruth couldn't get her sons to come to visit her, and the TV that they had given her became a substitute. She closed her eyes and she made believe that when hearing the TV she heard her sons talking to her. She listened intently to one of her son's conversations. She wasn't sure just what he was doing but she knew it was a shady activity. Ruth fell asleep and began to dream. She spoke to her elder son in her dream. "Son, could you bring some plants to the convalescent home?"

He replied, "What kind of plants do you want?"

"I would like some plants to beautify the convalescent home. Is that okay?" she said.

Her son, who usually didn't pay any attention to his mother, suddenly had a thought in his mind. "Mom wants plants. What a great place to grow plants. The residents will be busy and happy." He said to her, "Yes mom, I will get some plants and I will see you next week."

Ruth was dozing off in front of the TV. That was the only way she was able to communicate with her son: in her imagination.

The following week, still dozing and watching TV at the same time, she was surprised to see her son with not just one plant, but many plants. The plants were green and yellow, with big leaves. What a beautiful sight! Every resident got a plant. Even though the plants were small they were in five-gallon pots.

Her son said, "Mom, make sure that you water the plants every day and give them plenty of sunshine." Then he left the convalescent home.

Ruth was very happy. In her dreams her son had come to see her twice this month. She made sure that every resident took good care of his plant. Laura told her, "My plant is bigger than yours."

Ruth told her, "I watered it and gave the plant some of my cereals. The soil is soft and I enjoy feeling the wet soil."

Laura told her, "Tomorrow I will give my plant some eggs. What did you name your plant?"

"I call her Mary Jane."

Laura said, "I will call mine Mary Jane Laura."

Everybody gave their plant a name. Betty called her plant Mary Jane Betty. John's plant was Mary Jane John. Anna's plant was Mary Jane Anna. Bill called his plant Mary Bill. Bill, because of his heart condition, took many pills every day. He started giving them to his plant and it grew bigger and faster than all the others. Juana left out the "Jane" and called her plant Mary Juana, which she thought was very clever.

Laura loved her plant. She talked to it instead of talking to Ruth or Anna. She told her plant all of her secrets.

Ruth's son came every week to check the plants. They grew and became so big that they outgrew the pots. She told him, "Son, the plants have outgrown the pots; what should we do?"

"Mom, I will take those big plants and I will exchange them for small ones." He wanted those big, beautiful plants. You could see the greed in his eyes.

But Ruth was very happy with his answer. She had found a way to have her son visit her.

15

John and Myrna

John was eighty-five years old and a secret alcoholic. He had to drink in order to function. He started to drink at breakfast and ended just before he went to bed. At breakfast he had orange juice and whisky. During the day he sucked alcohol swabs. He had followed in the footsteps of his alcoholic father by starting to drink at an early age. This was the way he managed stress.

John also had Alzheimer's disease. Myrna, his wife, discovered it. She would send him to the grocery store to pick up some goods, and several hours later he would return, empty-handed. At the beginning he was able to come home, but later he would get lost.

He was married for sixty years, with two children and five grand-children. By the time I was there, he had been in the convalescent home for seven years. Myrna came to see him every day. She helped him wash, shave and dress. Sometimes she would take him home for a few hours.

John was a tall, well-built person. He had played football in high school and college, but he didn't make it professionally. Myrna, on the other hand, was short and skinny. They both had gray hair. Myrna, who was a year younger than John, had no intention of hiding her gray hair. They both wore spectacles and were nearsighted.

John had been a real estate broker, and he had been very success-ful due to his charming personality. Myrna had been completely depen-dent on him. She was a housewife. She raised her children, and when they grew and left the house she didn't know what to do. During the weekends John was busy showing houses to customers, and Myrna stayed home alone. He never called her. He used the phone in busi-ness all the time, but for calling home it seemed the phone didn't exist.

Then, after John had moved to the convalescent home, Myrna dis-covered garage sales. Every Sunday after church mass she went to garage sales. She would buy some trinkets. One day she discovered a hand woven shawl. It was a cashmere shawl. She tried it on. Suddenly, Myrna, her face filled with lines and wrinkles, became alive. She twirled the shawl around her shoulders and looked twenty years younger, like a Spanish dancer. The hand-woven shawl had many colors and embroideries. The owner asked Myrna if she wanted to buy it. Myrna answered shyly, "I don't think I can afford It."

"Make me an offer."

"Tell me something about the shawl."

"I bought it in India. I believe that the weaver spent his whole life weaving this one shawl."

Myrna made her a ridiculous offer, a very low price, but she really wanted the shawl. The owner accepted the offer. Myrna paid for the shawl and looked at it closely. It reminded her of her life with John. She was only a housewife, just like the weaver was only a weaver. They had both spent their whole life doing one job. Myrna took care of John and the weaver made the shawl.

She saw some blood spots, some water damage on the shawl. She wondered if the weaver had hurt himself weaving the shawl. Was he happy weaving the shawl? She remembered how John had mistreated her and how she had been dependent on him. She was happy that John was an alcoholic and had Alzheimer's disease. Now he was dependent on her!

Myrna remembered John's dilemma when they were in high school and he wanted to take her to the homecoming dance after the football game. The homecoming dance was the biggest dance of the school year. It was open to all classes, freshmen, sophomores, juniors and seniors. Many students panicked because appearance was very important and it was the biggest date dance besides the prom.

John had been a big football star. This was his last game of the year. The evening after the game was the big dance. Because he was a big football star all the girls were drooling over him. But John didn't have any money and didn't know which girl he was going to take to the dance. He decided to ask four different girls to the dance. He was honest and told them that he could only buy his own ticket to the dance, and that he would be taking more than one girl. In spite of this, all four girls accepted the invitation to go out with the football star. They bought their own tickets to the dance and treated themselves to dinner. John was able to rent his tuxedo and bought flowers for the girls so they could make their own corsages. Some of them made pin corsages and others made wrist corsages.

When John brought all four girls to the dance everybody was looking at him. It went to his head. He was the first person who had
brought four girls to the homecoming dance. They were tall and short.
They were blond and brunette. Some wore short dresses and some
wore long dresses. They all had a great time. John danced with all four
girls. Myrna, his future wife, was one of the girls.

Once John graduated from college he joined the army. Myrna
remembered that John was stationed locally. On his leave, he took
Myrna dancing. On the way to the dance hall he noticed four marines
driving around, looking for a fight with army guys. They approached
John and started to insult Myrna. In spite of the odds, John defended
Myrna's honor. They broke one of his arms and several ribs. Myrna fell
in love with his gallantry. A year later they were married. They'd had
two children: a boy and a girl.

Myrna's job was to take care of the children and John. John's job
was to provide for the family. Even then, John loved to drink. He was
drunk at his daughter's wedding. In this condition, he staggered to the
bar. The bartender had left the bar to get something. John wanted beer,
any kind of beer. Since the beer and the cold sodas were in a 50-lb
garbage can cooler, John tried to reach into the cooler to pick up a can
of beer. He fell into the ice and felt like he was frozen. He tried to call
for help but couldn't utter a sound. Finally, after spending six to seven
minutes in the ice-cold garbage can in a tuxedo, his wife found him.
Instead of pulling him out of the garbage can, however, she called the
guests to show them how her husband had made a fool of himself.

Through all the years of their marriage, they had been mostly at
odds. And Myrna had never found a purpose for herself, never felt she
was a worthy person...always dependent on John who, even as an
alcoholic, remained in control.

Now, with John in the convalescent home with Alzheimer's, the
roles were reversed. But his behavior was unpredictable. Some days he
was normal and she was momentarily able to forget he was sick. And
some days he was loud and couldn't stand any changes; if she moved
a chair he would start screaming. Other days he didn't even know who
she was.

John still drank heavily in order to function at all.

After so many years of feeling herself to be a nonperson, Myrna
had finally found her niche—of sorts. It was taking care of John. No
matter how he ranted and raved, no matter how bitter his complaints
or how blank his memory or how befuddled his mind from the alcohol...now he was dependent on her!

16

Laura and the $100

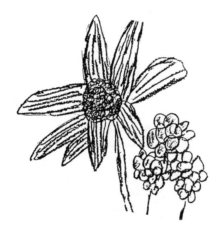

Laura was one of the most active residents at the home. She used every moment for living, and perhaps for this reason Oscar loved to be with her. Whenever he was there she read him stories and paid attention to him.

Laura dressed very colorfully. Her shoes matched her dress and scarves or sweater. Sometimes she wore a pink scarf with her blue dress, and sometimes she would add a blue sweater. She was full of life and humor. She was over eighty years old but only had a few wrinkles and didn't wear glasses. Although she had Parkinson's disease, she was very poised and graceful as long as she took her medicine. She used a wheelchair but, after doing exercises with Bill, she was able to use a walker. Laura had short, curly white hair and her skin was very white and glowing.

Every morning Laura had a hard time getting out of bed. She needed her medication to relax her muscles and allow her to move. Lying in bed helpless, just like an invalid, she opened her mouth, gulped some air, tightened her eyes and screamed to the nurse, "Where are my pills?"

Ruth, her roommate, also screamed, demanding Laura's medication. Finally Mary, the third roommate, got out of bed and got the nurse. Five minutes after Laura got her pills, she was able to crinkle her nose, hunch her shoulders, expel some air, shake her legs and, with the help of the nurse, get up out of the bed. She was shaking when she got out of the bed, and she was wobbling when she walked to the bathroom. Slowly she washed her face, brushed her teeth and used the toilet.

The medication was a miracle. Being stiff and unable to move was a nightmare. In the bathroom, Laura was able to sneeze and reached for a tissue, and that was a relief. The little things that we take for granted were her pride and joy.

Breakfast was a big ceremony. Everybody was happy to see each other at breakfast time-they had survived another night.

Laura loved eggs and toast, and the company of her friends. They discussed the daily activities that they were going to do, and all of the people that they would do them with. Maybe they would play cards or bingo, read a book or listen to a lecture. Laura helped Anna's grandson, Ben, do his homework, and discussed sports with him. This is why Ben insisted that his grandmother be friendly with Laura.

Laura loved to grow plants, and her room was filled with them. Her room had sliding glass doors that led out to the garden where she grew flowers and vegetables. The reason why she grew plants is because she didn't like artificial ones; she liked the smell and the beauty of the real ones.

Laura was always busy. Instead of wasting her allowance on cigarettes, she asked the nurses aide to buy her seeds or plants. She got twenty dollars a month as pocket money and took a long time to figure out how to spend it wisely. When you are all alone in a convalescent home you have plenty of time to think about how to spend your money. When the desires are many and money is scarce, what do you do? You cannot borrow when you don't have credit.

Laura loved the throw-away newspapers she got once a week. She was a good shopper and waited for sales. Out of the twenty dollars that she got, she gave five dollars to the nurse who gave her her medicine.

>─┤◀▶─O─◀▶├─◀

Laura had Parkinson's disease, a disorder of the nervous system

that reduces muscular control and causes severe shaking. Like in the
spring and fall when the clocks are changed, it was important to keep
to her biological time. She needed her medicine every eight hours. If
she didn't get it at the precise time, she started shaking and perspiring.
Katie, the nurse, didn't care. She was a little mean. She seemed to enjoy
people crying and begging for medicine.

Some of the residents didn't seem to care, because they were so far
gone it didn't make any difference to them. But Laura gave five dollars
to the nurse's aide, and saved five dollars for the beauty parlor. Every
month she needed her hair cut, a manicure and pedicure. With the five
dollars left, Laura asked Dora to wheel her to the drugstore. Five dollars doesn't go too far if you want to buy seeds or plants. She was
happy when the plants were on sale or when the manager of the store
was planning to throw some of the dying plants away. She asked him
if she could have some and he obliged. Back at the home, Laura nursed
them and brought them back to health. Laura bought a few packages
of seeds, like radishes, green onions and carrots. She knew that those
plants grow very fast, and she would be able to give them to her
friends. Oscar helped to plant them, and in a few weeks Laura would
be able to collect the fruit of her labor. Laura also had tomato plants.
Once you grow tomatoes you never get rid of them. Also, she had
some pumpkins growing.

Laura taught Oscar how to take care of the plants. He helped her
water the plants and soften the dirt. He thought it felt good feeling the
dirt and watching the plants grow.

Laura's garden was in the courtyard. At first the court yard was
filled with weeds and dirt. Laura started digging on her knees and soft-
ening the dirt. For days she worked in her garden, and suddenly it
became the place where everybody wanted to eat their lunches.

⊱┈❀┈O┈❀┈⊰

Laura's roommates were Mary and Ruth. Every first Wednesday of
the month, at two o'clock like clockwork, Ruth's son came to visit her.
She was one of the lucky ones. As soon as Ruth's son approached the
main door, even though she was far away from him, she felt his presence, not only with her eyes, but with her ears, nose, tongue and her
whole body. But in spite of the monthly visits, he made her feel like a
nonperson. She started to cry and nobody could stop her. Why did he
only come once a month, she wondered. She was always afraid that
this was the last time she would see him. Her son asked why she was
crying. He didn't realize that the moment he left she would become the

life of the party, laughing and having a great time-or so the nurse told him. He asked Ruth why his mother was crying. She told him she didn't know. Ruth was a Holocaust survivor. She had seen her parents being marched to the gas chamber, and she never saw them again.

Her other son never came to see her.

Ruth asked her son for some pocket money. He asked why she wanted it, if everything was provided for her. She begged him for some money. "I cannot live like a pauper. Remember, I gave you the house that you are living in."

"Yes, mom," he told her.

"I need cigarette money."

"Mom, don't smoke too much. You can burn the place down. "

"Son, why do I have to beg for money? I gave you all my savings. I need some money to tip the nurses or take my friends for a treat."

He gave her some money. While pulling a few dollars from his pocket he accidentally dropped a one-hundred-dollar bill. Laura happened to see it and raced over to it with her wheelchair. Suddenly she stood up, standing on the bill and hiding it underfoot. When Ruth's son had left, Laura called her nurse to help her pick up the hundred dollar bill. Laura was delighted to have a hundred dollars. It was a long time since she had seen such a bill. She asked her nurse's aide to change it to smaller bills and tipped her ten dollars. She felt like a big tipper.

Laura loved chocolate. In fact she was a chocoholic. She asked Dora, the nurse's aide, to wheel her to the nearby drugstore. While there she bought forty dollars worth of chocolate. It was Laura's big day. She was giving instead of receiving. She shared the chocolate with her roommates, Ruth and Mary, that night. They were sick for a week with diarrhea.

The rest of the money she spent on plants like marigolds, petunias, impatiens and others. After a month had passed, Laura couldn't hold her secret. She told Ruth, and Ruth laughed for the first time in months. Then, at his next visit, Ruth told her son about the hundred dollar bill. He forgave Laura. Laura was willing to pay him back, but he didn't want the money as long as he saw his mother and her friends having a good time.

Ruth told her son, "Will you please wheel me to the courtyard, and I will show you what Laura did with the money."

He took Ruth to the courtyard and said, "I can't believe what Laura has done. I remember the weeds and the dirt on the courtyard, and the rusted furniture." Ruth grabbed his hand and said, laughing, "You see what we can do with a hundred dollars."

"It's amazing. I know that Laura has Parkinson disease," he said.

Ruth replied, "She scrubbed and painted the metal furniture, planted flowers and vegetables. Now her work is complete."

Ruth told him, "This courtyard is my favorite place here. The smell, the pretty flowers and the vegetables make me happy."

Ruth's son kissed his mother, said good-bye and went home happy. He still came only once a month, but he felt he had chosen the right home for his mother.

The courtyard was now a lovely, comfortable place to sit. Laura had played a trick on Ruth's son by keeping his hundred dollar bill. There was some discussion among the residents about whether or not it had been the right thing to do, but most of them believed the outcome was worth it.

17

Mary

It was a source of wonder how Mary landed in the convalescent home. She lived only a few blocks away and she was happily married to an engineer. She had been a tap dance instructor at a local school. Mary was slim and tall, with small brown eyes. Her hair was straight and brown, with a smallish head. She wasn't a pretty woman; rather plain.

Mary was scared of everything because she had Alzheimer's disease and was aware of her poor memory. As you probably know, Alzheimer's disease is a degenerative disease that attacks the brain and results in impaired memory, thinking and behavior.

Her hands were always busy. She always held a piece of paper or a blanket which she would fold and unfold, over and over. She never talked. But sometimes she screamed if you approached her. Each morning, Mary took stealthy steps to the Lazy Boy chair, where she spent the day.

When her husband died Mary had fallen apart. She had lost her job and gradually she stayed more and more at home. She ordered Meals on Wheels and they delivered every three days. Her income was delivered to her bank, and the bank paid all her expenses.

By then, Mary was almost eighty years old. One day at home she fell and broke her hip. She had laid on the floor for three days. Nobody knew about her condition. When the delivery boy delivered her food, he noticed she had left the previous food outside the door. He knocked at the door. Mary didn't answer. The door was open, but was chained. The smell of urine and stool was very strong.

Mary needed an operation on her hip and it left her very weak. She stayed in the hospital as long as she could; the hospital couldn't send her home because there was no one to take care of her. That's how she ended up in the convalescent home.

Mary was placed in the room with Laura and Ruth. A week or so later, Laura and Ruth complained to the social worker about Mary. They didn't want her to be their roommate any more. Mary was a nuisance. In spite of her hip surgery, Mary was able to walk by herself, but Laura and Ruth needed their wheelchairs. Every morning Mary moved their wheelchairs out of the room and hid them. Sometimes she took and wore their clothes.

A meeting was arranged with their social worker. Laura and Ruth were there, but Mary didn't show up, so they started the meeting without her. Laura started by complaining that Mary was making her life miserable. "I have some nice clothes and I don't want Mary to wear my clothes and make a mess in my armoire."

Ruth added her complaints about Mary. "I need my wheelchair for transportation, otherwise I am a cripple. I bought it myself and I don't want anybody to use it."

The social worker responded by saying that Mary didn't have any problems with them or she would have come to this meeting. She told them if they were having problems with Mary they could move from the room

Angrily raising her voice, Laura asked the social worker, "Why do we have to move? Why can't we remove Mary from the room?" Laura was shaking; she could hardly breathe. The social worker gave Laura some water to drink to help her calm down, and then told them, "You see, you and Ruth are here and Mary isn't here. Where is Mary?"

"Mary is in the living room, sitting on her Lazy Boy chair, very happy." The social worker continued, "I can't help you. If Mary needs help and wants to change her room she would be here. So it doesn't do any good to complain to me, unless Mary agrees that there is a problem."

Ruth was sitting on her wheelchair, not speaking a word. You knew that any moment she would start to cry.

Laura told her, "It is okay, we'll just have to live with her."

One morning, instead of putting on her sweatsuit and getting dressed, Mary grabbed Laura's fancy dress and wore it. It was too short on her, but she didn't care. She also grabbed Ruth's shoes and purse; luckily, she wore the same shoe size.

Mary was going downtown, a five mile walk. She told the staff and residents that she had had enough of them. "Things have to change," she said. "I don't want some of the residents to be tied to a chair like animals." She was going downtown. The staff asked her how she was going to get downtown. She told them, "Very slowly." They asked her if she knew the way. She told them if she got lost she would ask some of the people for directions and they would show her how to go.

But Mary didn't leave the building. She completely forgot that she wanted to go downtown, and was totally unaware that she was wearing someone else's clothing. She walked to the dining room where she ate her hot cereal for breakfast. After breakfast she went to the living room and sat on her Lazy Boy chair, just like every other day.

18

The Day the House Died

Thursday was a troubled day at the convalescent home. The main goal of the residents that day was not to live well, but to just barely survive. If you took a tour of the home you would see that they were all taking many drugs that day, and they hit rock bottom. As long as they took drugs, they didn't cause any problems.

Ruth, who was usually always cheerful, was very down and sad. She didn't have the energy to get dressed and do her daily chores. When she did get dressed her clothes were very matronly, long, dark and old. Laura was in the same condition. Instead of her usual bright clothing, she dressed like an old lady: dark, unattractive clothes. It didn't look like her. She was sad.

Mary got up, got dressed, ate her cereal and sat on her Lazy Boy chair, staring into space.

Oscar came to the home and started nagging Bill to tell a story. Bill noticed that the morale of the home was especially low and told us all to gather in the dining room to hear him tell us a story. Maybe it was because Bill was a good storyteller, or maybe it was simply something to do, but almost all the residents gathered in the dining room.

These events that Bill was about to tell happened a long time ago. Bill started to tell about a house that was next door to his old neighborhood.

"Everybody in the entire neighborhood made jokes about the house next door, the way people make jokes about things they are unsure of. Many years ago this house had looked like a gingerbread house, like a fairy tale house. The red shingle roof was made of wood, but it looked like it was made of candies. People couldn't believe that this house was actually occupied. The rumor was that the house was made of candies, cookies and chocolate. The glass windows and curtains looked like cotton candy. The brick walls looked like a wedding cake decorated with caramel. The white brick fence looked like it was made of marshmallows and nougats. The gate was made of rosewood but it looked like two chocolate bonbons with nuts. The main door of the house looked like a big, brown cookie."

Laura said, "If the house was a gingerbread house I wouldn't mind grinding, nibbling and chewing the house."

Oscar was licking his lips and said, "Mmm! A big house made of cookies and candies."

Bill continued telling us the story. "The house also had beautiful landscaping. The bushes and the flowers looked like green jelly beans, and the trees were tall and majestic and enveloped the house with greenery. It looked like a happy, sunny and bright house.

"The house had the smell of a good housekeeper. The aroma was of fresh food, baked and cooked. In the morning you could smell the aromas of orange juice and rich cinnamon rolls, just baked with sugar and butter. In the middle of the day was the smell of onions and carrots. In the evening the smells changed to chicken or beef. All day long the aroma of fresh-brewed coffee wafted through the air.

Laura said, "With all this description of food, I'm getting hungry."

Oscar added, "So am I."

The nurse's aide brought orange juice and cinnamon rolls. Everybody grabbed them like it was their last meal. Bill continued telling us the story. "The thrill of the neighborhood children was to ring the doorbell of the house and then run away. They thought a ghost lived there, but there was actually a family living in this house. There were three people: a father, a mother and a son. The parents were quite old but their son was only twenty years old.

"The parents had enjoyed raising their son. They had dressed him in the latest fashions, and his parents made sure that he wore matching clothes: trousers, shirt, socks and shoes all matched. When he was young the kids had made fun of what he wore. He was always spick and span.

"Like their son, the parents took good care of the appearance of the house."

Oscar was all excited and he interrupted Bill, "Bill, Bill, if I rang the door bell I wouldn't run away like the other kids."

Bill petted Oscar on the head and told him, "Oscar you are a good boy." He continued telling us the story. "Both mother and father worked on the house every free moment. They cleaned it, washed it, and took good care of the landscaping.

"However, their son didn't help. He was young and wanted to have a good time. He refused to help with any housekeeping or gardening chores. One day there was a storm and a tree hit the house. It broke a window and destroyed part of the roof. If that wasn't enough trouble, at about the same time, the parents noticed that their son, whose age was twenty, always seemed to be tired, and frequently very thirsty-more thirsty than normal. They took him to a doctor and found out that he was a diabetic. As you know, diabetes, if left untreated, can lead to severe symptoms and even death.

"The parents took good care of their son. They tested his blood sugar, made sure he ate right, exercised and took his medication. As long as his parents took care of him he was healthy. And all the while, they also attended to the house. They fixed the roof and replaced the window. As long as they maintained the house it was well kept.

"As I said previously, the parents were quite old, and in the same year that the son's diabetes was discovered, they both died.

"After a while the neighbors noticed that the trees and bushes around the house needed trimming. Then the tree branches grew up against the windows and broke some of the panes, which weren't replaced.

"All this time the son ignored the house and it became dirty and run down. His own appearance had deteriorated as well, and he began to look sloppy, dirty and careless.

"The son told all his friends that he was tired of taking care of his diabetes, and he was going to take a vacation from being concerned about it. He was an insulin-dependent diabetic, yet he decided not to use insulin any more. He hated to give himself shots, and he hated to prick his finger in order to test his blood sugar. He also disliked exercising and enjoyed over-indulging in food and alcohol, all of which were bad for diabetes.

"One day there was a storm and a tree hit and broke the windows and damaged the walls of the house. When the first glass window broke, the son should have fixed it, but he didn't. Soon after, wind pushed the overgrown tree branches against other windows, and they broke as well. Broken glass was on the floor but he didn't bother to pick it up. The kitchen was a terrible mess, too, since the son only bothered washing one dish and one glass-the rest were scattered about, dirty and moldy.

"Meanwhile, the wind blew some roof shingles away, and the roof began to leak. Still he did nothing except drink more alcohol. As a result, his blood sugar climbed dangerously high and as a consequence of the diabetes, his vision became blurry and his feet and legs were very painful.

"The son's parents were long gone and there wasn't anybody to take care of the house and him. He had inherited some money from them, and as soon as he got it he spent it. He held elaborate parties, and served wine and beer to his guests. His friends were careless; they spilled the drinks on the floor and made burn holes by throwing down live cigarette butts.

"The son had totally forgotten his parents' values. He didn't take care of the house or of himself. Every morning he went to the bakery, and for breakfast he filled his stomach with the worst kinds of foods for his illness. He ate jelly donuts, chocolate donuts, any kind of donuts. He took some donuts home for lunch, and he drank three bottles of sugary sodas.

"From all the dirt and food lying around, roaches invaded the house. After the roaches came rats."

At this point, Bill paused for a drink of water, and Laura said, "I can imagine the house—how it must have looked after the parents died."

Ruth said, "Ugh! Roaches and rats!"

Laura added, "Probably there were spider webs all over, hanging from the ceiling."

Bill continued the story. "Yes, indeed, there were spider webs hanging all around the house and the son was drinking alcohol all day, every day, and his hands started to get numb. Sometimes his chest felt like an elephant was standing on it. Several times he passed out. Like the roaches attacking the food in the house, his disease was attacking him.

"There were flies in the house and several landed on him. At first he tried to brush them away, but little by little he got used to them. His heart was going too fast, then too slow, then fast. He didn't know what he was doing. He was just like a junkie. His friends that had come as long as he had parties had long since stopped coming. Now the house now smelled of fungus and mold. When his parents were alive, the house was warm; now it was cold. The once-lovely draperies were stained and torn.

"Through his dim awareness, the son sensed he was in real trouble. He wanted someone to come into his life and care for him, but now there was no one. He was on death row and so was his house.

"One stormy day, the wind caught the loosened roof and blew most of it off. Around the same time his heart stopped. He died on the floor in the middle of the mess he had created. There were no friends or family to mourn his passing.

"When I and the neighbors saw the house deteriorating, we should have inquired to see what was wrong. When the smell from the house became very unpleasant, we should have done something. But we didn't.

"That was the house next door to mine. The son died, and so did the house."

When Bill stopped speaking, everybody was quiet in the convalescent home dining room. Not a sound. Everyone was absorbing the story. There was a feeling in the room of deep sadness. By then it was lunch time. After first hearing Bill describe the wonderful smells coming from the house while the parents were alive, everyone had been hungry. But now they had all lost their appetites.

The nurses' aides pushed the wheelchairs to the dining room tables and served lunch. The residents faced their lunch and didn't eat. They were still quiet; nobody said a word, not even Oscar.

After a while, Laura was the first one to break the silence. "I was depressed before the story; now I am sick to my stomach."

But Oscar, who had heard a dozen or more of Bill's stories, suddenly said, "That was the best story I ever heard."

Bill smiled and asked Oscar, "Why?"

Oscar replied, "I like spooky stories. I was really afraid when he got sick and was dying."

Laura asked Bill, "Why did you tell us that story?"

Bill said, "The purpose is to encourage us to take good care of ourselves."

But the story did not have the desired effect. Bill's good intent had backfired.

19

Bill's Last Day

Oscar was sick with chicken pox. For a week he didn't come to the convalescent home, and during his absence, Bill died. One day in the middle of breakfast Bill grabbed his chest, suddenly turned blue, and fell to the floor. The paramedics said that he was dead before he hit the ground.

This was not uncommon in the convalescent home. At least ten to fifteen residents died every year, usually in the winter months. Bill died in the summer. It wasn't a hot day when he died, and when they eulogized him it was cool and pleasant. Very few people came to his memorial service at the home. You would think that after teaching school for so many years he would have many mourners, but very few people came to his memorial service at the home. His death was written up in the local newspaper. As a matter of fact he had written his own obituary. It read:

"To whom it may concern: I, William Young Thomas, or Bill Yours Truly, at the age of 71 years and __ months, wish to inform you that I passed away. Since I don't have any family or money, I want to be cremated and my ashes should be disposed of in the ocean. My clothes and my belongings should be sold and any money left after all my expenses are paid should be used for a Chinese banquet for my friends."

As it turned out, there was enough money for the Chinese banquet. My mother-in-law, Anna, and Laura, Mary, Ruth, John, Betty, some staff members, and my wife, Margaret, and I went to the local Chinese restaurant. The residents were all excited about leaving the home and going out for a treat. There were a total of twenty people: six in wheelchairs, twelve staff members and my wife and I. Margaret pushed her mother in a wheelchair and I pushed Laura.

Laura had been too long in the convalescent home and she was frightened to leave the shelter. I told her a hundred times that I would take good care of her, and she finally agreed to go. The restaurant was only a block away from the convalescent home, and when we got there it was empty-we had reserved the entire restaurant for Bill's party. The staff helped us to arrange seating and space for the wheelchairs. We had two large tables.

They fed us almond chicken, beef in oyster sauce, chow mein, sweet and sour prawns, won ton soup and rice. During the meal we had several toasts to Bill. The entire conversation was about what a wonderful person Bill was.

The food and service were excellent. The feast lasted for one hour. At the end we got fortune cookies. After dinner, everybody was tired, but happy. I helped take them back to the convalescent home. It had been a long day.

Several days after the dinner, when Oscar arrived at the home after his recovery, he ran to Bill's room. He wanted to show him his chicken pox scabs. He wanted to tell Bill how brave he had been and how he hadn't scratched his itchy rash. Oscar ran in and out of Bill's room. He noticed it was empty. He checked every room in the convalescent home but couldn't find Bill. He called Bill's name, "Bill, where are you?" Oscar felt terrible. He sensed that something terrible had happened to Bill. He asked Laura, "Where is Bill?" Se looked away and didn't say anything. Oscar kept nagging Laura, "I want to know, where is Bill? Please tell me, Laura."

Laura told him that Bill left the convalescent home to go to a new one because he didn't like it there any more. But Oscar knew the truth; he knew that Bill had died. He stormed out of the home.

I was afraid Oscar would never come back to see us again. The next day I went to his house and asked him if he wanted to go for a walk. I noticed that he was crying. "Oscar, were you crying?"

"No, I wasn't, I have a cold," Oscar said. All of a sudden, Oscar started to cry. I couldn't stop him. He sobbed and sobbed until I thought his heart would break. He asked me if we could call Bill or visit him. I told him the truth. Bill had had a heart attack and died. When Oscar finished crying he told me he remembered a story Bill had told him. I asked him if he would like to go to an ice cream parlor where we could talk. Oscar asked me why every time he was sad I gave him candy or ice cream. I didn't answer that, I just said, "Come on, let's go," and I took him to the ice cream parlor and ordered two milk shakes.

Oscar asked me, "Where is Bill?" I didn't know what to tell him. I told him, "Oscar, when you are older you will understand where Bill is."

Oscar sobbed again for a moment, then he told me he remembered a story Bill had told him. He began like this.

Once upon a time there was a father who worked very hard. Every day his eleven-year-old son would ask to play and he'd tell him that he was tired from a hard day at work. As soon as the father came home from work he plopped down on the sofa and drank beer. Then he ate dinner, watched television and went to bed. On the weekend he watched more television. He watched football games, basketball games, and baseball games. He never played with his son. His son begged him to play with him. He said to his father, "All the other fathers play with their children, why aren't you playing with me?" His father replied, "I'm tired."

The boy then asked his father how much money he made in a day. His father told him. The boy decided to hire his father for a day, so he could play football or basketball with him, just like the other fathers.

The boy started to work. He cleaned garages in the neighborhood. He mowed lawns, delivered newspapers, helped take groceries out to cars. Finally, after working very hard for several months, he reached his goal. He told his dad that he didn't have to go to work that day because he was hiring him. He showed his father the money and told him how he earned it. The father hugged his son, and tears sprang to his eyes. Suddenly he realized that time was flying by and that he was losing the most valuable years of his son's life. He told him that from then on he would play with him.

When Oscar finished slurping up the last of his milk shake, he finished his story. I hugged him and carried him home on my back. He told me he didn't want to go to his house; he wanted to be in Bill's room. I told him that Bill had left some things for him. There was a card. The card was addressed to Oscar.

"Dear Oscar: You are the son that I didn't have. I love you very much. Keep working hard. I believe in you and I know that if you put your mind to it you will be very successful. Don't forget the old people; one day you, too, will be old and forgotten. When you are older you will understand what I am saying. Remember me. I love you like a son. When you come to the convalescent home you will see many people like me. Remember us all. Love, Bill."

Bill had also left him some magnetic figures. I asked Oscar if he wanted to take them home. Oscar told me that he would rather leave them at the home. He asked me if I could find ten (pretend) telephones in the room. I thought I could see several magnetic telephone figures and after that I gave up. Oscar described nine magnetic pretend phones and said that with the real one that makes ten. Bill had helped Oscar learn how to count to ten.

From hanging around the convalescent home, Oscar knew about Parkinson's, Alzheimer's, heart attacks and CPR, and such. He asked me if we had given CPR to Bill. I told him we had done everything we could for Bill.

At that moment, Oscar saw Laura pushing her wheelchair into Bill's room. Angrily, he called her, "Puta!" (In Spanish, *puta* means prostitute.)

I asked him why he called Laura a puta. He told me, crying, "She lied to me." I realized that Bill meant a lot to Oscar, so I let him be angry. Oscar couldn't hold his tears. He asked me, "Do old people ever cry?"

I told him, "Yes."

"I never saw any of the old people crying." Oscar was yawning. Suddenly he got the hiccups, and I gave him a glass of water. Before sending him home I asked, "Do you know what the word 'puta' means?"

"No, but it is a bad word, and when somebody said this word to my mother, she got mad."

"Oscar, Laura didn't lie to you, she was trying not to hurt you. Please go apologize to Laura."

Laura hugged him and told him, "I am sorry that I lied to you, but in a way Bill did go to another home, maybe a better one, a home that is beautiful and calm."

Oscar was crying again. He couldn't control himself. This was the first time in his life that he faced death. Bill had been just like a grandfather to him. Oscar left Bill's room and went to the receiving room. He saw the mural and saw Bill's picture pasted on purple construction paper. Oscar asked me if he could have the picture. I took it off the wall and gave it to him. He grabbed it and put it under his shirt and ran out of the door.

20

Betty

After Bill died, the residents elected Betty to take over his job. She started consulting and teaching the residents. Nobody else seemed to want the job, and Betty who was an excellent pianist, was interested. There was a piano in the dining room. Once Betty got the courage to face the group, she started to play the piano during lunch and dinner and to read us stories.

Betty had several admirers, and one of them was Oscar. She let Oscar play the piano with her. At first Oscar hit the keys and made noise, but since he had an excellent ear for music, he actually started to play the piano with Betty. They both enjoyed each other's company. Betty never raised her voice at Oscar when she was teaching and playing the piano with him. They were laughing and giggling and acting silly. Betty had never had the time to play with her daughter when she was young; she'd had to make a living. Now she had the time and patience to play with Oscar. Her granddaughter was in college and never came to visit her.

The piano is a musical instrument that makes beautiful variable sounds. It represents a means of satisfying many musical needs within a single instrument.

Besides playing the piano she had a "consulting" job. She had Bill's office and every morning she "consulted" with the residents. She talked to them, and most important, listened to their problems. The residents were bickering among themselves about who got the best seat in the house. In the morning they wanted to see the sunrise and at night they wanted to see the sun go down. Betty took them from the living room to the outside of the building and assured them that it was safe to leave the building.

She also started taking better care of herself. She started losing weight, and instead of using her wheelchair she started to use a walker. She became happier, and wasn't thinking about her daughter. She started reading books and gave book reports to the residents. We all loved to hear her stories; she was a born artist. We all gathered together in the dining room. Betty started playing the piano and then told us this story.

The Heartless Queen

Once upon a time there was a queen who didn't have a heart. It is hard to believe that the Queen didn't have a heart, but she was heartless. It is true. This was first noticed when she was in kindergarten. She had many, many, many shoes: red shoes, black shoes, white shoes, green shoes, whereas some of her classmates had none. They asked her if she would like to donate some of her shoes to them. She told them if they didn't have any shoes, they should wear boots.

When she was in elementary school her heart still wasn't there. She had to learn to read and write since she was going to be the Queen. Some of her classmates didn't have pencils and crayons so they asked her if she would share her pencils and crayons with them. She told them to use chalk.

When she was in high school her heart still wasn't there. She had to learn chemistry, math, history, biology and civics, since she was going to be a Queen. She had beautiful dresses and some of the students asked her to give them her old clothes. She would rather destroy them than give them to her classmates. When some of her classmates were hungry and asked her for bread, she told them to eat cake. She didn't have a heart. She was heartless.

When the time arrived, she got married, but her heart wasn't there since she was heartless. She had three children: two boys and one girl to secure the throne. But her heart wasn't there. Her husband, the King, left her for a peasant woman who had a heart and loved him. He told the Queen he would rather be a peasant living with a woman who loved him, than a king living with a woman who couldn't love. The Queen's comment was, "Well, fine, then!"

Betty played the piano as accompaniment while she told us the story. Betty, herself, was sad that the queen didn't show any emotions. We all knew that the heartless queen was Betty's daughter.

Sophia, Ben and Oscar told Betty, "Don't worry, your daughter will come to see you." Betty knew better.

Every month the social worker evaluated all the residents and invited their families to attend the meeting. Out of the blue, for no apparent reason, Betty's daughter, whose name was also Betty, showed up at the meeting and then spent some time with her mother. But now Betty senior was as cold as ice.

Betty's daughter started visiting her mother regularly and wondered why her mother didn't want her company. The more Betty ignored her daughter, the more the daughter seemed to yearn for her company. She started coming every day and was hungry for her mother's love. She was looking sad and hurt and finally she had the courage to ask her mother, "Why are you neglecting me?"

The mother turned her face away from the daughter and didn't answer. Betty Junior faced her mother and said, "Mom look at me."

Betty answered, "I lost one child when I came to the home, but I gained many children here and they need me more than you do." Betty was serious when she said these words. Tears were in her eyes, but she controlled herself.

The daughter told her, "I was a fool, but please forgive me. I'll always have a special feeling for you."

Betty hugged her daughter and then she knew she had never lost her. Now they both realized that they needed each other. Betty and her daughter were crying. They shed happy tears, not sad ones.

Betty told her daughter, "You are a living legacy. Don't forget this. You are a part of me; my blood floats in your body. When you get hurt, I get hurt."

Betty's daughter asked her mom, "Would you like sometime to have dinner with me at my home?"

After a moment, Betty started crying. This time it was again happy tears. Finally, Betty answered, "I would love to."

Both women sat side by side holding hands. Not a word was said. It wasn't necessary. Betty knew that she had won her daughter back. They were sitting outside the building under the tree, feeling the cool air and enjoying each other, listening to the children yelling at each other from the next door apartments. The noise of the stereos, radios and televisions was loud. Betty's daughter kissed her. Betty Junior looked at her mother. Her mother looked back. No words were spoken, but they both knew something had changed. Something important had happened. A mother and daughter had rediscovered each other. Betty Junior turned and left. Both knew she would be back—quite soon.

One day, out of the blue, Betty told her daughter that instead of burying her in a cemetery she would like to be cremated. The daughter told her, "Mom, we are Christians and you should be buried in the cemetery next to your parents."

Betty replied, "If I was buried in the cemetery I wonder when you would come to see me, but if I was cremated and my ashes were scattered in front of your favorite department store, I would be sure that you would come to visit me every day."

Betty junior was quiet; she didn't say a word, but she knew in her heart that her mom was right.

21

Time Running Out

It was Sunday afternoon and Anna wasn't feeling well, and it was time for Margaret and I to visit her. My daughter, Sophia, had a few hours before going to work, so she decided to join us. My son, Benjamin's, soccer game was canceled because of rain, so he also decided to visit his grandmother.

Anna told us she couldn't sleep last night. She said she was very tired and she looked exhausted. Her eyes were red and her hair was a mess. The noise of the rain had kept her awake. She had put her head on the pillow but nothing happened. She had told herself to be quiet and go to sleep. Then she called the nurse to fix her bed, and the nurse straightened the sheets and made the pillows fluffy. Normally at this time Anna would be snoring. Instead she heard the clock ticking: tick-tock, tick-tock. Everybody else was asleep. She wondered what was wrong with her. She couldn't wait for morning to come so she could see us.

It was raining on, rain again, neither a cold rain nor a hot rain. It was only raining, raining and raining. When it rained, the residents liked to cuddle themselves in bed because they were hungry for the sun's heat. They felt the sun gave them energy, and so when it rained the residents didn't feel like doing anything. The sun gave them the will to live. The nurses' aides liked the rain, and they didn't encourage the residents to leave their beds, because it was more work for them when they did.

Oscar came to the home. He was running through the place. He was the only one who was full of energy. He wore his new tennis shoes, navy blue shorts, a light blue T-shirt and his baseball cap. He begged Laura for a story. It had been a long time since Laura had told him and us a story. Oscar nagged her, "Please, Laura, tell us a story. There is nothing to do today. We can all go to Anna's room." Finally Laura agreed, and we all gathered in Anna's room.

Anna and her roommates were in bed. Laura was sitting in her wheelchair. Sophia, Ben and Oscar were sitting on Anna's bed—all four of them. Anna and Sophia were sitting in the back kind of lying down, and Ben and Oscar were in front of the bed. Margaret and I took two chairs near Anna. She was very quiet, but alert. Laura was ready to tell the story.

Tick-Tock, Tick-Tock

"Once upon a time there was a beautiful Queen. She was blond with green eyes. She lost her husband and became a widow. She should have been happy, since she was the queen, but she wasn't. Her husband, the king, wrote a will. In the will it was written that the queen must marry in a year's time; otherwise she would lose the kingdom. Her kingdom consisted of a small country, a throne, a palace, money, clothes and jewelry. She had a year, and the time began to pass. Tick-tock, tick-tock, tick-tock.

When the single men in the kingdom heard about this they decided to approach the Queen. There were tall men, short men, skinny men, fat men, bright men, stupid men. You name it-every kind of man was there. The Queen was having a wonderful time. Every night she went out with a different man.

All the men tried to impress her. They took her to fancy restaurants, to wineries, to concerts, to the circus. Months and months passed. Tick-tock, tick-tock.

Every man was trying to out do the other men. After all, the winner would become King. Now the time seemed to be flying by. Tick-tock, tick-tock.

Finally it was the last day of the year. On that day a poet arrived at the palace to try to win the queen's heart. He dedicated poems and short stories to her. He flattered her with beautiful descriptions of her pretty face and graceful body. The queen knew If she didn't marry by midnight she would lose her kingdom. Tick-tock, tick-tock.

She agreed to go out with the poet. He didn't take her to an expensive restaurant; rather, he took her to a dump. He told the Queen that this restaurant was all he could afford. The queen became very angry. Tick-tock, tick-tock. She was so angry she forgot all about the deadline for her to marry.

The clock stopped. The next morning she lost her kingdom and became a poor woman."

When Laura had finished telling us the story, Oscar started repeating, "Tick-tock, tick-tock, the clock is ticking."

Benjamin asked Laura, "Is this a true story?

"Is it really about someone you knew?" Sophia asked.

Laura was quiet for a moment, then in a very soft voice she told them that she was the queen. 'When I was a young woman I wasn't interested in dating. Everything else was falling into a pattern. I had my work, I had my house, and some good friends. All of a sudden I met a man who was after me. We dined and danced, and he wanted to marry me. I got cold feet. I asked myself, 'Why do I need this?' and I let him go."

Sophia asked Laura: "Do you regret that you didn't marry him?"

"Yes, I do. He married my best friend, and I lost both of them."

>-+-+>-O-<+-+-<

It was still raining and we were afraid to leave Anna. Anna assured us that she was okay and we should go home. The other residents were all in bed, asleep. The quietness was like magic. Nobody made a sound. You could blame it on the rain.

The staff would rather keep them in bed, in diapers, than help them out of bed. It was more work to get them out of bed, to dress them, wash and feed them and to take them to different activities. Once they started to stay in bed they became passive, without life.

Most of them wanted to end their lives. They were thinking about one word. It was "sleep." Seeing the residents in bed in the middle of the day was painful. Sophia, Ben, Margaret and I gently tried to got the residents out of their beds. We told them to listen to the clock, ticking the time away.

Meanwhile, it was raining, raining and raining. Anna was now out of bed. She was sitting in her wheelchair. Ben wheeled her around the corridor. She fell asleep. We left her sleeping in the wheelchair. The clock was still ticking.

22

The Good Son

David was the doctor for the residents of the convalescent home. In five years he was planning to retire, at age sixty-five. He was happily married and had three children who were already grown up and out of the house. His wife had been a social worker before raising her children. Now she was retired and they had no children to take care of.

Twice a week David's wife volunteered to work with the residents while David treated them. At the convalescent home she talked to each patient. She asked them how they felt and encouraged them to talk about themselves. She held their hands, listened to their complaints, combed their hair and made sure that they looked presentable for the doctor.

It was very important that she visit each resident first. Once they felt comfortable and at ease, the residents didn't mind being checked by the doctor.

David was my mother-in-law, Anna's, doctor. She enjoyed the visits from the doctor and his wife. He made Anna smile and gave her hope. He told her about his children and about himself. If he went with his family on vacation, he mailed her postcards from exotic places, like Bali, Jakarta, and Singapore.

David felt he owed a lot to society, and the way he paid them back was by taking care of some residents free of charge, in addition to his regular patients that he charged.

David had been born to alcoholic and drug addicted parents. His father had left him when he was three years old, and his mother died of a heroin overdose when he was six. He spent his youth in foster homes. When he was in junior high school he had stolen some money from the cafeteria. He wasn't caught but then somebody squealed on him. A few months later he stole a bike. The judge at

Juvenile Hall didn't know what to do with him.

In the courtroom the dirty-faced young man stood before the judge with tears in his eyes. The judge was ready to place him in a reformatory for a year. Instead, the judge had a friend who was a doctor, and he asked him if he would try taking David home, to see if he could straighten him out. The judge knew that David had never had a father to teach him right from wrong, or a mother who could properly feed and clothe him.

With the support of a large, loving family, David quickly shaped up and became an outstanding citizen. He graduated with honors from high-school, college and then from medical school.

The judge had believed in David. If a child like David is given a decent place to live, wholesome meals, clothes and love, the child has a good chance of becoming a responsible, substantial citizen. If David had gone to the reformatory instead to a loving family he'd be in the penitentiary now.

David never stopped searching for his father. Before she died, his mother had given him a gold necklace with a medal, and on the medal was his father's social security number. He found out that his father collected social security and he wrote to that address, but all the letters were returned. He tried calling him, but there was no answer. He went several times to the flophouse where his father was supposedly living but he never succeeded in finding him.

One day a new resident came to the convalescent home, who had been sent from one of the local hospitals. He was quite old and the hospital felt they could do no more for him. Everybody was excited because the new resident had the same first and last name as David. The coincidence was absolutely remarkable. David was very excited, hoping he had finally found his father.

David, the elderly patient, was very weak and sickly, but still you could see some resemblance. He was tall and slim. He had a full head of gray hair. His eyes were gray and he had a flat nose. When you looked at him what you noticed first was his beautiful gray hair. David, the doctor, didn't have the same nose, but he was about the same height, slim, and also had a full head of gray hair.

Doctor David started taking good care of him. He fed him, helped him dress, and washed him. Perhaps it is strange that a doctor did all those things, but Doctor David was very excited and grateful that he had finally found his father. When he spoke his name, elder David didn't reply. Doctor David thought that his father was just weak and as soon as he got his strength back he would be able to acknowledge him as his son.

"David, how are you feeling?" the doctor asked the patient David.

The patient didn't answer at first. Then he told the doctor, "Don't call me David."

"Isn't that your name ?" the doctor asked, and tried to reassure the patient that his name was David.

The patient told him, "Please don't call me David. That isn't my name."

Doctor David gasped and couldn't make a sound. Tears were in his eyes. He felt as though once again he was the boy in front of the judge, but this time he thought that he was in front of his father. He stared at his father and felt pretty shaky.

Doctor David was still convinced that the patient was his father, but didn't question him further. He brought his family to the convalescent home so they could meet his father. Later when Doctor David's family had left, the patient told the doctor that he wasn't his father. His name was phony and so was his social security number. He told him, "I lived with your father at a cheap hotel, and when your father died I took your father's social security number, since he got a bigger check than me. Also, I donated your father's body to the medical school. Maybe you dissected him when you were in medical school." Doctor David felt ill and left the room.

Nonetheless, Doctor David continued visiting the patient who was using his father's name. He brought him clothes, magazines and food snacks. The patient continued to deny that he was Doctor David's father. But Doctor David believed that his father was ashamed and had made up his story about switching names.

Patient David lived another two years at the convalescent home before he died, and during that time Doctor David and his wife continued to care for him. Doctor David always believed that the man was his father.

23

The Birthday Party

Laura, who had Parkinson's disease, was dressed colorfully. She loved bright colors. She wore a flower-printed dress, a navy blue scarf and black shoes. She looked very festive. She was ready for Oscar's surprise birthday party. She was very happy.

Laura's roommate, Ruth, was dressed in pink, and wore a straw hat with flowers plus sunglasses to protect her from the sun. She was also ready for the party and she was proud that Oscar had grown so much.

Mary, the third roommate, had Alzheimer's disease. She wore her yellow sweat suit. She hadn't any idea what was going on, but she seemed happy enough sitting on her lazy boy chair.

Across the hall from Laura, Ruth and Mary, was Betty and Anna's room. Betty finally had the great occasion to wear her new pink dress and her white patent leather shoes. She combed her hair and used some make-up and was ready for the party.

Betty had a special rapport with Oscar. Oscar was fascinated by the

piano, and he would sit on Betty's lap on the piano bench. He would-
n't make a sound. Betty would take Oscar's hand and lead him to play
the piano with her. If he only played for a few minutes you had to tell
him how great he was.

One of the residents, John, also had Alzheimer's disease and was a
secret alcoholic. When John wasn't drinking he was consuming chocolate. Sometimes John shared his chocolate with Oscar and some of the
residents. When he was drinking he told Oscar he was taking medicine,
but Oscar knew better. The alcohol smell reminded him of his father
who also drank heavily.

Before he died, Bill had told me how John had landed in the convalescent home. John was a successful real estate salesman, married for
sixty years, with two children. If you saw him and his wife you would
think they were still on their honeymoon. They always held hands, and
he wasn't embarrassed to kiss her in public. But one day, after sixty
years of marriage, John informed his wife, Myrna, that he wanted to
leave her. He had reconnected with his high-school sweetheart who
was living in a trailer park 100 miles away from their home.

John told his wife she could have everything except his social security check. He left for his adventure and lived for two months with his
new sweetheart. Things began to sour, though. The woman began to
yell at him and he became morose. He called his wife and asked her if
she would take him back. After much persuasion on John's part, Myrna
reluctantly agreed. She realized that he was an alcoholic and that the
Alzheimer's disease was getting more serious. Shortly after their recon-
ciliation, she put him in the convalescent home where he had now
been for two years.

Myrna came every day to visit him and sometimes she would take
him home for a few hours. Myrna would rather have a husband than
be a grass widow, even though John was sick and couldn't remember
much.

One day, Oscar informed all the residents that the next day,
Wednesday, August 31st, was his birthday. He was going to be five
years old. After Labor Day he would start kindergarten. He let the residents know that he wasn't going to have a party, because his father
didn't get paid until Friday, and the family had no extra money for parties.

A birthday isn't a birthday if you don't get a special cake and a present. Laura, Ruth, John and Betty decided to surprise Oscar. John collected the money for the party. With his poor memory, John asked
some to pay twice and others not at all, but they still trusted him to collect.

At that time my mother-in-law, Anna, was very sick and was being fed in bed, but she wanted to participate, so I wheeled her in for a little while. Sophia decided to wear her old cheerleader outfit and cheer for Oscar. John bought toys and decorations for the party, with all of the money that he had collected.

On Wednesday, everybody was ready for Oscar's surprise party. John shaved and wore his favorite T-shirt. On the T-shirt was printed:

At my age
I've seen it all
I've heard it all
I've done it all
I just can't remember it all

The residents asked the cook to bake a birthday cake and cup cakes. He did, and decorated them with sparkle candies. They also got soft drinks and vanilla ice cream. Vanilla was Oscar's favorite flavor.

On Wednesday, Oscar came to visit the home. He was sad and mad. It was his birthday and his father had left for work early without wishing him a happy birthday. His father was a gardener and his mother was a cleaning lady. When she was working she left him with the next door neighbor. Oscar's mother was worried that Oscar was on the street and unsupervised, so she decided to send him to a babysitter. His mother told him the family would celebrate his birthday on Friday. He'd get a birthday cake, a toy and new clothes for school.

He entered the building without saying a word. He dragged his feet and he was dirty. He was crying and you could see the dried tears on his face. He rubbed his eyes with filthy hands and had a running nose.

Laura greeted Oscar, "Good morning, Oscar."

Oscar didn't answer. Once again Laura said, "Good morning, Oscar." Her voice was low and sweet. Again Oscar didn't reply.

Ruth asked Oscar, "Did you tell me or Laura 'good morning'?"

Still Oscar didn't reply. Then Laura and Ruth left the room. Finally, Oscar started to talk to them but he didn't realize they had left the room. He was the only one in the room. He talked and talked to himself, complaining about his birthday and about his parents. "It isn't fair, it is my birthday." He was sobbing, his cheeks and his eyes were wet with tears. The more he talked, the better he felt. Now he felt good enough to wonder where everyone was. He started toward the dining room.

Before Oscar could open the door, Sophia and Ben came up to him, blindfolded him and took him to the dining room. He heard Betty playing the piano and everybody singing. They were singing "Happy Birthday"—to him!

Oscar was still blindfolded. When they removed the blindfold Oscar was on Cloud Nine. The room was decorated, there were cakes, soft drinks, cup cakes, and presents. Sophia lit the sparkling candles on the cake and Oscar was able to count them. There were six candles, five for his age and one for luck. Everybody was still singing. Oscar couldn't wait for the song to end and blew out the candles and thanked us. He said, "I wish Bill was here." Sophia cut the cake and Oscar helped serve it.

I looked around the room. There were smiles everywhere, and more than a few perplexed expressions, as if the septuagenarians, octogenarians and a few nonagenerians were trying, hard, to remember what it felt like to be five years old, but could not quite do it. I laughed, mostly because it made me remember a time when getting older was actually a thrill.

Laura asked Oscar, "How does it feel to be five years old?"

Oscar replied, "I don't know. I know that today I am five years old. I know that I am old enough to go to school."

Laura lovingly looked at Oscar and said, "Oscar, I know that you are going to be a good student."

Oscar told Laura, "When I push your wheelchair, I feel like I'm older than five years. When I sit on Mary's lap I feel like I'm one year old. When I wet my pants I'm two years old. When I work in the garden with you I am ten years old. When I remind Katie, the nurse, about your pills, I'm a big person. When I crawl on the floor I act like a baby."

Laura agreed with Oscar. She said, "Sometimes I feel like I am a hundred years old. Other times I am a little girl. Oscar, life is complicated."

But not for Oscar. He was happy celebrating his birthday. He thanked everybody again. Anna had not been well enough to stay at the party for long, so Oscar went to Anna's room and told her about the party and showed her the presents. He got coloring books, crayons, wooden blocks and metal cars. I knew that time was running out for Anna, and so I let her eat the chocolate cake in spite of her diabetes.

Oscar told everybody, "Eat the cake and ice cream slowly so it will last longer." He filled his plate and made a glutton of himself. His eyes were bigger than his stomach.

Laura asked Oscar, "What did you like most about the birthday party?"

Oscar was jumping and acting silly. "I liked everything!"

Then the party was over. Oscar was very tired by this time, and he started to cry. One minute he was happy and the next minute he was sad. Oscar informed us that he wasn't coming to see us anymore. Why couldn't he come to see us? In the morning he had to go to the babysitter and now in the afternoons he was going to school.

Before Oscar left, Laura asked Oscar to hug everybody. It was hard for Oscar to say good-bye. He dragged his feet and he was sad. He didn't want the day to end.

He asked Laura, "Is my birthday party over?"

"Yes, Oscar. If you want, you can hug us and say good-bye."

Oscar hugged John first, than Mary, Betty and Anna, then several others. The last one he hugged was Laura. He hugged Laura for five or ten minutes and then he told her, "You are my abuelita." (Abuela means grandmother; abuelita sweetens it as a term of endearment.)

I helped Oscar to take his presents home. From that time on, the old people didn't see Oscar anymore. Every morning the residents of the home pushed each other so they could have the best view from the glass door, hoping to see Oscar. Once again they were forgotten people, people without a face.

The days became longer and more monotonous for Laura. Laura remembered that every afternoon after her nap Oscar was there. She had planned her days around him, reading him books, telling him stories and working in her garden. She would ask him to water the plants.

Now he was gone and her days were terribly long. She really loved him. She felt like part of her was being cut off. If she saw another child at the home she called him "Oscar."

Laura said to herself, "Fine, I'm okay. Fine, I'm okay." She didn't cry. She didn't get angry. She just went numb.

Betty had enjoyed teaching Oscar to play the piano. Now she played mechanically, without feeling.

Mary sat in her lazy boy chair, holding a blanket and pretending it was Oscar. She kept whisperir.g, "Oscar, Oscar," kissing the blanket, folding it over and over again. She kept crying, holding the wet blanket to her face as she hugged it with her two arms wrapped around it. The blanket was dirty and smelled of food and urine, but Mary didn't let anybody take her blanket.

Oscar was a chapter, a moment in the lives of the forgotten people.

24

Anna

When Anna died it was a great loss for the whole family. Anna was our chief and leader, and when she died the last of a whole generation was eliminated. My own parents died early and so did my father-in-law, and so Anna had been the matriarch for a long time and the family had revolved around her. We all knew that we could turn to her for security, comfort and wisdom. Now Margaret and I had become the big chiefs. In my tradition, the eldest is the family leader. Now we had to make the important decisions, like where we were going to live, what kind of work we would do and about our children's future. Leadership is a difficult task, especially when it is handed to you at the same time that you have lost a loved family member. I was frightened by our loss, but began to prepare for the inevitable.

The loss of Anna made me remember how I had met my wife. It was February 4th, my mother-in-law's birthday. Her family had gone to celebrate Anna's birthday at a restaurant. There was a musician who played the violin, and a palm reader was also present. The family challenged her to read Margaret's future. The palm reader, after looking at her hand, told her about a dance that she should go to because there she would meet her future husband. Margaret went to the dance. I met her there, and I also met her best friend. The following week I took her best friend out. We went out to a Chinese restaurant and to a comedy show. I thought everything went well, but it didn't. My wife's best friend called her and told her what a terrible time she'd had with me. I hadn't been polite—I hadn't opened the door for her, either at the restaurant or at the car. I had walked in front of her.

When she finished complaining about me, Margaret must have thought I was awful. The next day I called Margaret and asked her if she would like to go bowling. In spite of her friend's poor opinion of me, Margaret remembered the words of the fortune teller and she accepted. Five months later we got married. My mother-in-law, Anna, supported me all the way. She told my wife that I was the right one for her. Two years later I became a father. My mother-in-law came to help my wife take care of the baby, but she was more of a moral support than helping hands.

One night my wife and I decided to go to the movies. We tucked the baby in and left her in the family room. We turned on the television and told Anna to watch the baby. My mother-in-law took the order seriously. She sat and watched the baby. She didn't move from her seat. Two hours later when we came back she was happy to see us. She'd had to go to the bathroom but was afraid to leave the baby alone. Little by little we trained Anna to take good care of our daughter. By the time my son was born she was an excellent babysitter.

I remember the day my son, Benjamin, was born. Anna, who wouldn't drive in the rain, came to see us. She looked like Mary Poppins, with her black coat, hat, umbrella and a grocery bag filled with food. Anna decided to cook. She was making a Russian borscht. Borscht is a beet soup that you eat hot with sour cream. My wife ate it but felt nauseated, and we knew that it was time to take her to the hospital. Two hours later my son was born. At that time it was the policy of the hospital that only the husband could come to visit the mother and child. Anna was dying to see her grandson, so I tried to smuggle her into Margaret's room so she could see her daughter and grandson. She was so noisy that they kicked us both out of the hospital.

Our children enjoyed being with their grandparents. They loved to stay overnight and weekends because their grandparents bought them clothes and toys, and played cards and dominoes with them. Margaret and I enjoyed the peace and quiet of being alone.

Three things I learned from Anna about relationships. The first is that life is too short, so don't fight. And never to go to bed angry. Go to bed in peace because you never know if you are going to wake up the next morning.

The second is to change roles with the one you love. Maybe his or her way is better than yours.

The third is, don't eat meals with the television on. Family conversation is best around the dining table.

Holidays and birthdays were very important to our family. Anna loved to cook but she was very secretive with her recipes. My daughter, Sophia, enjoyed helping Anna cook so she could write down the family recipes. For my birthday, Anna prepared my favorite meal: beef Stroganoff, which is tender beef slices in a delicately flavored sauce with mushrooms and onions, topped with sour cream. The sauce made the meal, and it was Anna's secret. She made us delicious soups like borscht, barley and spinach. She also baked cakes and cookies for the children.

The enrichment that my children received from their grandmother, Anna, I can't describe. Anna was always for Sophia and Ben. My daughter remembered her grandmother as peacemaker. She hated fighting with her brother, either verbally or physically. Anna told Sophia to look at him as though he was the only one she had, that one day her grandparents and parents would be gone. Anna said, "The most important concept is that being together the two of you can conquer the world. Separated, you both are losers."

I remember one incident that happened to Ben when he started Sunday school. He was in first grade and he enjoyed going to Sunday school. He met a friend, Frank, and even though they didn't go to the same public school they enjoyed each other's company at Sunday school. They had the same interests; they liked to play sports together, especially soccer. They played on the church team.

Both boys played the fullback position. Ben, being a lefty, played on the left side and Frank, being a righty, played on the right side. They used to call each other on the phone often, and talk for a long time.

One day Ben invited Frank to his birthday party in May. Frank didn't show up. The following Sunday when Ben saw Frank at Sunday school, he complained, "Why didn't you come to my birthday party?"

Frank replied, "My parents couldn't take me to your house."

Ben continued to be friendly with Frank. The school year ended and they didn't see each other till the following year. They continued their friendship. Ben invited Frank to come to his house several times but Frank never showed up. But still they played soccer, basketball and baseball for the church.

The next year, Ben invited Frank to his birthday party. Ben told Frank, "Don't forget to come to my birthday party."

Frank replied, "Don't worry, I'll be there."

The party started and Frank wasn't there. Ben was sad that his friend once again hadn't come to his party. Next Sunday Ben brought cup cakes to Sunday school for the class and brought some little gifts for Frank. Ben asked Frank after giving him a cup cake and the gifts, "Why didn't you come to my birthday party?"

Frank didn't look at Ben and then blurted out the truth: "I wanted to come but I couldn't! My parents told me not to associate with you!"

Ben frowned: "Why not?"

Frank looked away. He felt inhibited because he didn't want to hurt

Ben. Then he said, "Ben you are poor, and my parents don't want me to associate with poor people."

Ben felt that he had been slapped on his face. "I never knew that I am poor."

Frank said, "Yes, yes, yes you are. You don't go to private school, you go to public school. You live down the hill and I live on top of the hill. Your mother and father work. We have a maid, a nanny and a chauffeur."

Ben didn't say a word to Frank. After Sunday school Ben didn't come home, he went to see his grandparents. He was crying. He asked Anna, his grandmother, "Are we poor?"

Anna gave Ben some cookies and milk and told him, "Ben, first sit down and enjoy your snack."

"Grandma, are we poor?" Ben asked again, this time more urgently.

"Ben, who told you this nonsense?" asked Anna.

"Grandma, I invited my friend to my birthday party and he didn't come. Then I saw him at Sunday school and he told me he didn't come to my birthday party because we are poor." Ben went on to repeat all of Frank's words.

Anna grabbed Ben and told him to sit on her lap. She hugged and kissed him and then she said, "We aren't rich in money, but we live comfortably and our richness is in having a loving family."

Like all the other times, at this time in Ben's life, his grandma was there for him. She comforted him and gave him advice. Ben continued to go to Sunday school. He didn't associate with Frank anymore, and although Ben was unaware of it at the time, his friend, Frank, was being picked up by the chauffeur and walking in to an empty house. His father was a doctor and his mother was a high society lady who was busy doing charity work. In contrast, Ben had a home where both parents and sister were there for him, and a grandmother that never let him down.

Sometimes I wish that time stood still and didn't cause change. Having the whole family together eating, laughing and telling each other good stories is one of my fondest memories. But life is always changing. After a year in the convalescent home, Anna began to deteriorate rapidly. Her kidneys were not functioning. We knew that she needed kidney dialysis. This was dangerous at her age because she had had several heart attacks while she was on the dialysis machine. A short time later, Anna had died.

My wife and I took the death of Anna very hard. We went to a support group focusing on grief. The group met once a week at the hospital where Anna died. We were looking for a miracle cure and fast healing. We thought the social worker would have some magic to take the pain away from us, but we were wrong. There isn't any magic in healing the pain of losing someone you love; only time heals.

Our first meeting started with a social worker and ten people: seven women and three men. Most of the people were couples who had lost a parent. The social worker greeted us, and started by telling us to take a big breath of air and inhale and then exhale. Then we introduced ourselves. Then she asked us, "How big is your pain?"

I wondered how you can measure your pain. We went around the room, and each one gave her a number for their pain. If the number was smaller she'd praise you; if the number was larger then she'd scold you. She told us that next week she expected us to do better. The following week we didn't show up. I didn't want to cry in front of a room full of strangers.

I thought about each day as it came along; whatever happens will happen, and before you know it a day passes, a week passes, a month passes, a year passes and time alone heals the pain and wounds.

We managed to go on living. Little by little, the sharpness of the loss dulled and I was left with a shadowy sadness which is always present. I will never forget my mother-in-law, but the particularities of our life together began to fade.

When we buried Anna, I noticed that my wife, my daughter and I were all crying. We let her go, but my son had a hard time handling it. He couldn't cry, he just kept it inside. I asked him how he felt about his grandmother. He told me she was a unique person. "She showed me how to fight my battles. I remember at elementary school the other kids teased me and hit me. She told me first try to avoid a fight, but if that didn't work, fight hard. Surprise the enemy, kick him, bite him and punch him, all at the same time. It only takes one good fight, and you gain the respect of all the classmates."

While telling us that story, Ben slowly began to cry, first with a little tear, then great big sobs. After a while he calmed down.

Anna had been the matriarch. With her death the title was passed to my wife, Margaret, and life went on.

25

Margaret, My Wife, My Love

A few years had passed since I last visited the convalescent home. My mother-in-law, Anna, had died, and so I thought I didn't have any reason to visit but I was mistaken. One doesn't need a personal reason to go there; there is always something to do.

Before my visit I thought I knew everything about the home, but after visiting it this time, I realized I didn't. Those people need companionship and helping hands. The staff at the convalescent home were only able to provide physical care, not love and affection. Families didn't always visit as often as was needed.

I remember it was a Tuesday morning when I finally loaded my station wagon to the brim. I filled several large, black bags and took them to the convalescent home. As I entered, the old gang was sitting by the entrance of the home: Laura, Ruth, Betty, John, Myrna, Rita and Mike.

Laura was the first one to recognize me. She said, "What brings you here, stranger?"

I answered, "I brought something for the home."

Ruth shook hands with me but then angrily said, "The mystery man is back."

"Don't get upset. Why are you getting upset?"

Ruth replied, "Why not?"

"Don't start quibbling with me," I shot back.

Ruth looked at me angrily and replied, "Your mother-in-law died and you never came back to see us."

"Ruth, I just arrived here and you immediately started quibbling with me. Why don't you let me greet the rest of the residents?"

"Why should I? I want to talk to you and tell you what's happened in my life." She grabbed my hand and she didn't let it go. Her hands were cold. I felt they were the hands of an old lady that had poor blood circulation.

I asked if she was cold. She didn't reply. I was finally able to free myself from her grip and I went to greet the rest of the residents. I asked the staff to help me unload the station wagon.

They helped me bring in ten black bags.

Laura, who was curious, asked me, "What did you bring us?"

I didn't answer. I was irritated. I had brought the bags and now I wanted to leave them and go home. I told myself, I have nothing to do with these people. They are old and sick. I had paid my dues years earlier when I visited my mother-in-law frequently.

The staff interrupted my thoughts. They told me to empty the bags and display them on the tables in the dining room. Once displayed, I distributed the things among the residents.

I had lost my wife several months ago, and all of her things like clothes, shoes, purses, etc., had remained in the house. I had promised her that I would donate them to the convalescent home, but for a long time I couldn't do it. My daughter tried to help me by gathering the clothes and putting them in plastic bags. I just left the bags in the extra bedroom. It was as though Margaret was away and she'd be back soon. It was very hard to accept that I had lost the one that I loved.

When I buried her, at first I was the center of attention. But as the days passed I found myself alone. I ate by myself, I dressed by myself and I slept by myself. When I started going to the grocery store, I bought for two but ate for one. Then I realized that I was really alone. At the grocery store my friends tried to avoid me. I asked myself what crime did I commit? Is it contagious?

I went to church and nobody wanted to sit next to me. Everybody was whispering behind my back. Then I went home and I was all alone again. At that point I realized that she was dead and she wasn't coming back. Margaret had told me to give her clothes away, and now I thought that the poor people at the convalescent home could either use her clothes themselves or they could have a rummage sale and use the money they earned to buy bibs and diapers. I brought the clothes and distributed them among the residents. You could see how happy they were. I brought sweaters and coats. It was pretty cold outside, and they could use them.

It was just like Christmas. They were so happy. Each one of the female residents found something of Margaret's to wear. I gave Laura a dress and a coat. The dress was colorful. It was made of wool. I told her it would keep her warm. She thanked me and told me that now she would be able to go outside. I only gave Betty scarves and purses, since none of Margaret's clothes fit her. Ruth tried some dresses and this was the first time I saw her laughing and happy.

All the residents were shy, but despite their pride they accepted the clothes gratefully.

All of sudden, instead of seeing Margaret, I saw many Margarets. I remembered each garment; when she had bought them and when she had worn them. But instead of feeling sad, I became happy. Seeing so many happy people with her clothes resurrected a part of her.

Some people asked me to tell them when Margaret had bought the clothes, and when she had worn them. I told them, and shared the events. The memories were beautiful, and sometimes funny, but all were filled with life. It was the first time since Margaret had died that I felt happy.

26

The New Year's Card

Holidays are the saddest time of the year for some of us. This year, Christmas was a week away. It would be my first one spent alone since losing my wife six months ago. After thirty-two years of marriage, she died of cancer. I have two adult children. My son asked me to spend the holidays with him, but I decided to spend them alone, rather than be a burden to anyone.

I felt lonely remembering our Gulf of Mexico cruise. This was the last good time Margaret and I had together. We enjoyed the time alone and the company of some of the passengers. One woman kept my wife company while I was at the gym, and they became good friends.

Before my wife died, when she knew she hadn't long to live, she asked me to call this same woman, Cecilia, whom we had met on the cruise. Margaret thought that she'd be perfect for me. Cecilia had lost her own husband three years ago, and there were many things we had in common. We both loved to travel, read books, and watch musicals. We both had children the same age, a boy and a girl. Perhaps my wife was right.

After six months of mourning, I finally found the courage to call. I left her a message: "Hello, this is Alex," I said nervously. "I wonder if you remember me from the cruise?"

Cecilia called me back right away and asked if my wife Margaret was okay because the tone of my voice had worried her. I informed her that I had lost my wife, and I asked her if she had noticed that my wife was sick during the cruise. She wasn't sure, but she had enjoyed my wife's company. "Now I remember," she said, "you never left the ship, but you were so eager to hear about our land excursions." Then she came right out and asked me if I was dating. I told her no. She said she had a man in her life, but he didn't mean anything to her. "He is very generous and takes me out to fancy places, but he's not the same religion as me." I smiled at that. I was the same religion.

I mailed her a New Year's card and expected a reply from her; that was the way I was brought up. But she never replied. I called her before Christmas, and she said she couldn't talk, but after the holidays she'd call. I didn't really know her very well, but in spite of that I got jealous and sent her a bouquet of flowers, signing the card, "A secret admirer," with my telephone number. On Christmas day she called, thanking me for the flowers. Her voice was warm and friendly. I was caught like a fish, suddenly filled with romantic feelings.

"Why did you ask for my address the first time we talked?" I asked her.

"I was planning to mail you a New Year's card," she said.

I was in heaven. I imagined that she was going to mail me the most beautiful card that anyone had ever seen; or perhaps it'd be a carefully made, delicate one wishing me a better year. Or even better, she'd order a hand-painted one. Or she'd use my name with every letter some joyous message. Maybe something like:

A bold New Year filled with peace, health and happiness
Love and joy for the holidays
Especially for you, may your New Year be filled with happiness
Xmas that's filled with peace, health and happiness
Signing the card: Love, Cecilia.

Now I couldn't wait for her card. December 25th passed, then December 26th, December 27th, December 28th, December 29th, December 30th. I waited every day for the New Year's card. I told myself, the mail is slow; any day I will get my New Year's card. After all, it's not a junky card. She may be still shopping for it. I called her December 31st to wish her a Happy New Year. I asked her how her holidays were. She talked and talked and talked, complaining about her boyfriend. I thought perhaps I had a chance. She was staying home for New Year's because her boyfriend was on a yacht race.

I asked her if she ever got a kiss on the phone. I was dying to kiss her. I told her to press her lips tightly and say "prune." I was in heaven. We were kissing! She told me I had tricked her.

A week passed and obsessively I checked my mailbox every day but I never got a New Year's card from Cecilia. Sometimes I walked to the mail box five or six times a day. Maybe the card got lost. The flowers that I had sent her had probably died and, I had to admit, so did my love for her.

This wasn't exactly puppy love—it was old dog love. This was the woman my wife had chosen for me, and so it was hard to accept that it didn't work out.

I felt sorry for myself. I went to the park and sat on a bench staring at the other lonely people and pigeons. An old man came to feed the pigeons and asked if he could share the bench with me. I nodded a yes. He gave me some bread. I was hungry and I started eating it. He told me the bread wasn't for me, it was for the pigeons. Then I decided to leave the park and I went to the convalescent home to be with the less fortunate ones, the ones that we have forgotten. The ones that also didn't get New Year's cards. The ones who are tirelessly waiting for their children and grandchildren. I decided to come every day to the convalescent home. To eat with them, push their wheelchairs, talk to them and just be with them.

27

Amy and Sophie

The first time I saw Amy and Sophie I fell in love with them. Amy and Sophie are dogs, both Bichon Frises, two affectionate pets. They are very small. At birth you can hold them in the palm of your hand and they only get to be eight to twelve inches tall and weigh twelve to fifteen pounds. Their fur is snow white. I still cannot pronounce their fancy name, which sounds something like *Bee Shaman Free Zag*. My daughter, Sophia, left them with me to babysit. She and her husband were going on vacation, and Sophia informed me that it was time to leave the house, to open the curtains, remove the sheets from the mirrors and start to live. It had been six months since my wife died.

Amy and Sophie looked at me with their begging eyes. All they asked for was food, water, and love. The first two were easy, but the third was hard. It meant not only fondness; you must brush them, clean their waste and take them for walks.

As soon as I touched their harness they knew we were going for a walk. I wondered who was the master, even though they were so small and you could easily kill them by stepping on them, they still had control of me. They pulled and pulled me. I told them, "Amy, no!" "Sophie, no, don't pull!" They were so happy to leave the house, so peppy and energetic while taking a walk. I taught them not to pull on the leash. If they surged ahead, I snapped the leash and told them "No." I rewarded them for walking nicely beside me.

I found out that dogs eat poop. They weren't shy or finicky—they ate anything. Amy ate Sophie's feces and Sophie ate Amy's feces. The only way to stop this was by walking them on a leash and picking up after them immediately.

After their walk they fell asleep. When I lay on the sofa, crying and thinking about my wife, Sophie jumped on me, licking my tears. It felt good knowing that they were thinking about me. They were a great comfort to me.

Lately, I was going to the convalescent home to work with the residents. It beat sitting in the park feeding the pigeons. I wondered what reaction I would get from the residents if I brought Amy and Sophie. So the next time I went, I drove my car and the dogs sat next to me. They whined. They wanted to stick their heads out of the car window. They wanted to feel the wind ruffling their fur and smell all the scents of the world. I was worried that they would get carsick and vomit, so I opened the car's window a little and I let them smell the fresh, cool air.

The first time, I smuggled Sophie into the convalescent home and left Amy in the car. Sophie received a royal welcome. Laura, who was afraid of animals, let Sophie sit on her lap. She had just eaten a poached egg. Some of the egg was on her upper lip and she let Sophie lick it. When Sophie finished licking, Laura was in heaven—she didn't have to wash her face.

Once I noticed it was safe, I brought in Amy, too. I let most of the residents pet the dogs. The dogs were running and chasing each other, entertaining the residents. Everybody wanted to feed them. The residents almost killed the dogs by giving them chocolate candies and chocolate cake. Amy and Sophie weren't too shy to eat the chocolate. I took the candies from them and washed their mouths. Chocolate for dogs is like us eating plastics. It will damage our stomachs because we can't digest it.

Amy and Sophie were running from room to room. They were sniffing the residents. They were looking for food. They were investigators at heart. They used their noses, ears, eyes and mouths, and they loved to chew. At the home they only found worn-out shoes and clothes. There weren't soft stuffed toys or bones to chew.

Amy caught a paw on a wire and unplugged one of the oxygen machines. Luckily, I was there and fixed the damage quickly. Now I know why they don't allow us to bring pets into the convalescent home.

After a while, it was time to go home. The residents asked me to bring the dogs every day. I was sorry to say no; there was too much likelihood of them causing serious troubles. Their visit was only a tease, but better than nothing.

I brought the dogs home. They were exhausted and flopped down on their bellies and went to sleep. Before they went to sleep I heard them barking. If you couldn't talk you would probably bark, too. I told them to be quiet, but they had something to say to each other. I didn't interrupt them. Amy and Sophie got excited and that's why they barked. I shouldn't yell at them. I should listen to their conversation. They were talking about me. "He's a very, very boring conversationalist; all he knows is: 'Amy, sit. Sophie, eat, fetch,' and 'no.'"

Finally, they went to sleep.

The next day my daughter returned from her vacation, and picked up the dogs. It was too short. It was also a tease.

28

Cecilia, Another Tease

As a young man I was always fascinated with the mystery of the ocean. I enjoyed swimming with a group of friends. One time we started as a pack and all of a sudden I separated from the group. I was swimming in the ocean and when I dove down I saw a green light. Then the light of the sun hit my eyes and I almost became blind. The only relief I got was when I dove into the ocean and I once again saw the green light. Diving down ten feet I saw a cave. I wasn't afraid to penetrate the cave. The green light had come from a pair of green eyes. The green eyes that I saw reminded me of Cecilia, who was the woman I had met on a cruise.

Months ago, Margaret, my wife, and I went on a cruise. She was dying of cancer. She told me, "Alex, promise me that when I die you will get married again. You and I are married for eternity, but I want you to continue living."

I replied, "Please don't talk about death; let us enjoy the cruise."

"Alex, I have very short time to live and you have made me very happy and I want you to be happy."

"Margaret, we will find a cure for you and we will live together for-ever."

Margaret didn't respond to that. Instead, she continued, "Alex, have you noticed Cecilia?"

"Yes, Margaret."

"Alex, she is beautiful, smart, a widow, the same social economic status as us and very well educated."

"Margaret, please let us talk about the cruise and forget about Cecilia."

This had only happened six months ago. Now, the green eyes seemed to call to me to explore the cave. I continued downward until I was inside the cave. Surprisingly, there was an air pocket at the top of the cave and I was able to breathe freely.

It wasn't dark inside the cave. I was amazed that there was so much light. It was coming from the huge green eyes, which provided enough light so that I could see colorful fish and beautiful corals. The ocean outside was restless but the cave was calm.

All of a sudden I saw Cecilia. Her blond hair was weaving in the clear water. Her green eyes looked at me. I could hear her saying, "Come in, let me show you around." Her lips were red. I wanted to kiss her. I wanted to hug her. She was giggling. She dared me to come clos-er. I was all excited. I was going to an unknown territory.

I had broken the diver's law when I had separated from the group. Diving is fun, but I shouldn't have been alone. I was afraid, but the sense of adventure was exciting. Seeing Cecilia was a treat. Then I looked at the green eyes and I realized that it was a moray eel, five or six feet long and weighing about 160 lbs. Moray eels are carnivorous.

The eel grabbed my fin. I pulled my leg but without success. All of a sudden another eel grabbed my waist and tried to strangle me. I start-ed fighting it. I had a spear and used it. I shot the spear inside the body of the eel, but the eel turned out to be a giant octopus. It had eight long tentacles which are used for crawling and picking up things. I was the thing.

I was able to get loose. I was able to swim and leave the cave. Tears were in my eyes. I was happy to be alive.

A few weeks passed and I still was thinking about Cecilia. It was like a sickness. Should I call her, yes or no? I picked some daisies in the back yard and pulled off the petals, saying, "I'll call her, I won't call her." Even after counting one hundred daisies, the result came up, "I'll call her." So that's what I had to do.

"Cecilia, this is Alex." I said.

"How nice of you to call." she said sweetly.

I told her I had written a story about her. "You're kidding," she said, "I don't believe you." So I read it to her: "The Greatest New Year's Card." This is a true story, I told her. A woman teasing a man by promising to send him a New Year's card. The card was never mailed. The man was grieving the death of his wife and was looking for sympathy and a loving hand.

Cecilia said the story was only partly true.

"What do you mean?" I said, "Did you mail me a New Year's card?"

"I did buy you a New Year's card," Cecilia said, laughing.

"But I never received it," I said sadly.

"I was planning to mail you the card on Christmas, but Christmas passed. Then I was planning to mail it on New Year's day, but New Year's Day passed. Now I am planning to mail it to you on Valentine's Day, with my picture."

I asked her not to mail it to me. I didn't want her to have the last word. But a week later I got a letter with her picture. I found her outstandingly beautiful: blond, green eyes, wonderful smile. I called her to tell her how gorgeous she was. She told me that nobody had ever called her gorgeous, only beautiful or pretty. I thought we were getting along nicely.

She asked if I could come in a month or two to see her. I was flattered and getting more and more anxious to see her.

If I drove it would take a whole day; flying only one hour. Next month I flew and she met me at the airport. Everything that I had imagined was true. She was almost the same height as me. She wore black pants, a yellow blouse and a black, fancy vest. She looked like a million dollars.

I had a sign which read "Cecilia," but I didn't need the sign. She had recognized me right away. I gave her a kiss on the cheek, although I should've given her one on the lips. We went to the beach and had a romantic walk. At first she let me hold her hand, but she was teasing me. She held my hand and then she dropped it. She told me it was too soon to hold hands; let's just be friends. I was on cloud nine. We walked on the beach barefoot. We felt the cool, gentle waves and we tried not to wet our clothes. It was hot and she took off her vest. I noticed that she had lost a button from her yellow blouse. I imagined the softness inside. I couldn't help notice that she walked in a way that made her hips turn with each step...beautiful...provocative—at least to me.

We went to one of the large hotels for lunch. It was Sunday and they were having champagne brunch. Cecilia was happy. She fit right in with the plush dining room. Once at our table I immediately began dreaming. This will be a perfect place for our wedding. Bob, her deceased husband, will be the best man, and my deceased wife, the maid of honor. My son and her son the ushers; our daughters will be the bridesmaids; her grandson the ring boy. Cecilia will probably wear her wedding dress. I will wear my tuxedo, the one I wore to my daughter's wedding.

The waiter brought me back to reality, asking if we wanted champagne. Cecilia ordered a glass and I declined. I had orange juice. She asked me if I drank. I told her no. "How boring!" she exclaimed.

She opened her purse and showed me some pictures of her family: her son, her daughter-in-law and her grandson. Her grandson was a two-year-old blond kid and he looked just like her. He wasn't fat but full; you could see that he was not an active kid but a good sitter.

Her son was also heavy and needed to lose some weight. Her daughter in-law was a petite brunette and slim. I wondered why she didn't show me pictures of her daughter. I guess she tried to protect her from a single available man.

We ordered salmon, and after we had eaten I asked her if she wanted to read some of the stories that I wrote. She did and she cut them apart, nit-picking them and totally missing their beauty; only pointing out the spelling mistakes and grammatical errors.

I felt awful. All I saw was a red pencil in her hand marking my mistakes. I was afraid to show her any more of my work. She destroyed my creativity.

After lunch we were already tired of each other. We were speechless and we had nothing to say to each other. I guess we were on a different wavelength.

She took me back to the airport. I realized that she wasn't the woman for me. I flew home with tears in my eyes. I wiped my nose on my arm and I wished I had a soft tissue paper. I wondered how my wife could have made a mistake by choosing Cecilia as a new wife for me.

I was angry and I asked Margaret, "Why did you choose Cecilia for a wife for me?"

Margaret replied, "Give her time. Maybe you will learn to love her."

"Margaret, I am not a child and don't treat me this way," I said.

Margaret replied, "Well, I guess you have to live your own life, now, and make your own choices."

And this is part of the healing process.

29

Learning the Hard Way

When Cecilia called me I stopped everything as though I were hypnotized. She was coming to see me-to spend a whole day with me! It seemed impossible that I was still interested, but I guess I was like a beaten and obedient dog. The master hits the dog and the dog cries. Then the master pets the dog and the dog is happy. The master hits the dog again and the dog cries again. Then the master pets the dog and it is happy once more.

When my wife died I lost the most important thing in my life. Now, in my suffering, if anyone was kind to me I felt grateful to him or her. Cecilia was again acting kind toward me and I fell for her. She was coming on Saturday to spend the day with me. When she called me on Friday to give me her flight number, she asked what my plans were.

"Do you like Spanish food?" I asked.

She said she liked paella and gazpacho.

"Cecilia, I will prepare them for you."

"Alex, don't go to too much trouble," she said.

Completely ignoring her, I spent the whole day cooking the paella. The smell of onion, oil, tomato, garlic, rice, chicken and shrimp was overwhelming. This was going to be a paella to remember—worthy of my love to Cecilia. I was dreaming of how I'd fix the table. Should we eat in the kitchen or the dining room? I decided on the dining room. I put the best linen cloth on the table, the best china and silverware. I was imagining that the four of us were eating dinner together: Cecilia and her deceased husband, Bob, and Margaret, my deceased wife, and myself.

I heard Margaret tell me, "Alex, please hire Sonia, the cleaning lady, to serve the food."

I answered, "Of course I will hire her to serve dinner. I don't think Cecilia will feel comfortable being alone with me."

"Alex, don't forget to serve wine," reminded Margaret.

"But I don't drink, you know that!" I said, rather annoyed.

"Alex, but Cecilia drinks wine."

"Which wine shall I serve, red or white?" I then asked.

"Open two bottles, a red one and a white one, and ask her which one she would like," said Margaret.

The first dish was to be a papaya cut in half as an appetizer, then the gazpacho, salad, and the main dish, the paella. For desert, coffee and French pastry. I thought that I would be able to win her not only with looks and intelligence, but with my cooking, too.

I picked Cecilia up from the airport. Once again she looked great, and once again she began to dictate the situation. I gently informed her that she was my guest and it was my responsibility to show her a good time. I showed her my house which is only five minutes from the airport and told her that we'd be having dinner at my house before she flew home.

I took her to a romantic fishing village where the men were just returning with their catch of the day. We chose two fish which the local restaurant cooked for our lunch. We walked around the city holding hands and I thought Cecilia was as happy as I was, walking on the beach, visiting galleries and tourist shops. We spent several hours like this laughing and talking about nothing in particular.

One of the galleries had some of Picasso's art works from the war years and we went in to see them. There was a reproduction of his famous painting, "Guernica." Guernica was a town in Spain that was destroyed in 1937. Picasso painted the horrors and destruction of that town.

Cecilia wasn't interested in seeing it. She wished we were in the wine country, drinking wine. I reminded her that I don't drink and I said we should just enjoy the paintings. There were some impressive original paintings from the late 30s. "The Weeping Woman" and "A girl with a Cock" were two that I especially liked. Cecilia softened a little when she saw the painting of a mother and child. I told her that Picasso first painted the child and later added the mother. I wanted to show off my knowledge. She seemed impressed. After an hour in the gallery I saw a slight smile on her face. Perhaps she was enjoying herself after all.

It was getting close to dinner time and so I headed us toward my home. Cecilia was apprehensive. She told me that there were thousands of restaurants we could go to and that she didn't feel comfortable eating in a bachelor's home. I told her that my cleaning lady would be with us. But she told me to call Sonia and tell her to go home. Instead, she named one of the most expensive restaurants in the city but I refused since she wasn't going to pay the bill. Instead I took her to a Mediterranean restaurant where they had music and dancing.

I noticed Cecilia was angry. Her face turned red, and she shut her eyes, as though ready to scream. I could see a smudge of dark red lipstick on her teeth. I told her to take a breath of air and count to ten, just as you'd do with a child. I felt she hated me because she didn't get her way. She had wanted to go to the wine country and to an expensive restaurant for dinner. She'd heard about vineyard tours that take three to four hours and include wine tasting with cheese and fruit. She was disappointed with the day and with me.

After dinner I took her to the airport. I was also angry because I had worked very hard to make the dinner which we didn't eat. I didn't even get a thank you. Next time she whistles, I thought, I hope I don't run like a good puppy.

I called her the next day, more out of courtesy than anything else. I was wondering how she was, how her flight was and if she had arrived home safely. Her answering machine was on and I didn't have the courage to leave a message.

She never called me again, and I never called her. I guess I will learn to live without Cecilia.

I still had my mission to visit the convalescent home. Time will heal as long as I am busy, and I was busy in the convalescent home, keeping the residents company, making sure that every morning most of the residents got up from bed, ate their breakfast and went on to different activities.

I suppose having Cecilia coming to visit me was better than nothing; at least it was a diversion.

Visiting the convalescent home and helping residents gave me the will to live, and to learn from my mistakes.

30

Lunch at the Deli

After my morning of volunteering at the convalescent home, I decided to go to lunch at a local Deli. Since my wife died, I had been grouchy and very touchy. Everything irritated me. Having to deal with people in a store or restaurant was an ordeal, especially when I was hungry.

I went to the Deli, and waited for ten minutes to be seated even through the place was half empty. Finally the hostess with the mostest approached me and asked, "Where would you like to be seated? Smoking or nonsmoking?"

I didn't want to be seated in the smoking section where the smoke would get all over my food, so I said, "Nonsmoking, please." She handed me a menu and I was seated.

A few moments later the waitress approached me and asked me if I made up my mind. I ordered a diet coke and potato pancakes. The waitress took my menu and I thought she took my order, but a few minutes later she came back and asked me again if I wanted a menu. I told her I already ordered a diet coke and potato pancakes. She asked me if I wanted apple sauce or sour cream, and I told her both. She said that it would be extra if I took both. I said, "Okay, I will pay extra," starting to become annoyed.

I was sitting, waiting for my lunch. I called to the waitress and asked if I could have my drink. She brought me a coke. I asked her before taking a sip if it was a diet coke. She told me that I had ordered a coke and corned beef sandwich. I informed her that I ordered potato pancakes and a diet coke. I could feel my face start to flush. I told her to forget about the food, and I got ready to leave. She handed me a bill for the coke. I left without paying. On my way out I heard her say to the hostess, "Those old people don't know what they want."

The next day I told my son, Benjamin, the story. He took me back to the restaurant and told me to be patient. The restaurant was again half empty. We waited ten to fifteen minutes again to be seated. The same waitress came to take our orders. She was tall, had bleached blond hair and wore a green uniform. I was dreaming of the potato pancakes with applesauce and sour cream. In the dream the potato was fried nice and crisp, and the applesauce and sour cream melted in my mouth.

I ordered potato pancakes and a diet coke. Ben ordered the same. The same waitress told us, "You don't want this. It's not good for you. I will get you fresh orange juice and corned beef sandwiches. You don't want a chemical drink and fried food." I looked at Ben and told him, "Let's get out of here."

I went home with my son. Ben doesn't live with me any more. I told him that I owed him a meal. I told him that I would make him potato pancakes. I peeled some potatoes and an onion. I grated the potatoes and onion and I put it in a blender with water, eggs, one spoon of salt and 1/3 cup of matzo meal. I heated oil in the frying pan and added the mixture and fried the potato pancakes. Ben and I enjoyed the company and the meal.

Now that I am alone I must clean the house, cook and take care of myself. Part of healing is standing on your own two feet.

Sometimes people will be nice to you and sometimes they will not.

31

How Dorothy Met Peter

I noticed that the nurses were always in a good mood in the convalescent home, no matter how sick the residents were. They laughed, giggled and tried to make the patients happy. But when the patients don't feel well and don't have the support of family or friends, they are doomed. They don't have the will power to live, and they die quickly.

One of the residents was a lady who was ninety-two years old. Her name was Dorothy. Even at her advanced age she was in excellent health, tall and slim and very alert. Every morning she drank tea, ate toast and read the paper. She loved to read the personals column: women seeking men, men seeking women, men seeking men, and women seeking women. She asked one of the nurse's aides if she should write to the paper, looking for a man. The nurse's aide encouraged her to write and see what might happen.

Dorothy read one of the ads to the nurse's aide: "Professional, 54-year-old woman in search of romance; be willing to lie about how we met."

The nurse's aide's name was Virginia. She was a widow and she, also, was 54 years old. She told Dorothy, "Read me more of those ads."

Dorothy continued reading. "A complete package. Beautiful inside and out, feminine, blonde and blue eyes. Looking for the perfect man."

Virginia looked at Dorothy and said, "Do you believe her? I wonder how old she is?"

Dorothy continued reading aloud. "A+, passionate and very attractive, slim, 5'6", Mediterranean-looking brunette. If you like to dance tango or salsa get in touch with me."

And then there was: "Attractive, voluptuous, sexy, smart with sense of humor, style and class, only 38 years old. Enjoys fine dining and fine wines. Seeks tall, healthy, relatively fit man, 45-55."

Virginia looked at Dorothy and told her, "Dorothy, I believe that you can do better."

Dorothy grabbed her stationery paper and pen and started writing: "Dorothy seeks an honest relationship with an elderly man, who has a sense of humor."

Dorothy printed her ad and got a number; whoever wanted to get in touch with her had to refer to that number. She got fifteen responses. Some of the men asked her how old she was, if she was wealthy, a widow, divorced, and what kind of morals she had. Dorothy noticed one letter that stood out from the rest. It said, "Dear Dorothy, I am an elderly person with a wonderful sense of humor and would love to meet you. However, I stutter. Would you please consider meeting me? Sincerely, Peter."

Dorothy showed the letter to Virginia and asked her, "Should I answer the letter? I am so nervous, I feel like a teenager. Virginia, why don't you answer the letter for me?

Virginia said, "Dorothy, you started this; now finish it. Pretend to be sixty years old."

Once again Dorothy sat down, picked up her stationery paper and started to write. She wasn't trembling, and her handwriting was straight and legible. "Dear Peter: Out of fifteen letters that I got the first day, I picked yours. Before I commit to meet you I would like to know something about you. Yours, Dorothy."

Dorothy couldn't believe it. She kept getting more letters, and by the end of the week she got a second letter from Peter.

"Dear Dorothy: It isn't easy to write to you. I have never done this before, answering an ad from the paper. What can I tell you about myself that I can win your heart? I am a 62-year-old school teacher, 5'10", brown hair and brown eyes, physically active. I must have a good sense of humor since I have been teaching for forty years. I am a widower. I lost my wife two years ago. I am new at the dating game but I hope we will meet soon. Yours, Peter."

Dorothy was excited that she was corresponding with a secret admirer. She didn't know what to write to him. The next day she got another letter from Peter. "Dear Dorothy: Every day we pass by attractive people of the opposite sex. We don't want to be rejected. We're all scared to death of rejection. I am mailing you a self-portrait picture and I hope it will speed our relationship. Please tell me something about yourself. Peter."

Dorothy showed the letter and the picture to Virginia. Dorothy told her, "Isn't he handsome? He shouldn't have any problems meeting any women. I better write him right away."

She wrote: "Dear Peter: I am very sorry that I didn't write to you sooner. I am a 60-year-old widow. I still am working as a nurse. I am also eager to meet you but please don't rush me.

You are a very handsome man and you shouldn't have any problems dating. Yours, Dorothy."

She mailed the letter and inside she put a plastic bag with a potpourri.

The next letter from Peter said, "Dear Dorothy: Do you think it is too early to start dating after being a widower for two years? My wife was my high-school sweetheart. We got married after college graduation. I am a teacher and my wife was a dental assistant. We didn't have any children—only a German Shepherd dog named 'Butch.' Since I lost my wife, Butch is a great comfort to me. Do you like animals? Thank you for the potpourri. I keep it in my jacket and keep thinking about you. Yours, Peter."

Dorothy showed the letter to Virginia and asked her what to do. Virginia told her, "This is getting out of control. Sooner or later he will ask you to meet him. Tell him you found somebody else and ask him to forget you."

Dorothy told Virginia, "This is exciting!. This is the only thing that is keeping me alive! Before this relationship life was boring. I got up in the morning, relieved myself, took a shower, ate my breakfast tea and toast, and read my paper. Now I am alive, making history instead of just reading it. I am going to tell him about myself and ask him about his work."

"Dear Peter: I do love animals, but I never had any because my husband was allergic to them. Five years ago I lost him to emphysema. My life is very simple. I get up in the morning and have my breakfast toast and tea. I go to work at the hospital. Have brunch-a fruit. If I am lucky I have lunch at 12 o'clock: salad, toast and tea. Three o'clock is time for yogurt, and for dinner at six o'clock, chicken, steak etc. in front of my TV. On week-ends, if I don't work I visit my friends and we go to ball games. I love baseball. I hope this year we will have a winning team. Please tell me about your job. It must be an exciting job. Yours, Dorothy."

"Dear Dorothy: I am also a fanatical baseball fan. When the baseball season starts I am glued to the television or in the ball park. I teach five periods a day, 200 students, age 14 to 18. The classes are mixed boys and girls. I have several mentally retarded students in my classes. I have a problem that I hope you can solve for me. I have a student, a 14-year-old, who is retarded. The kids at school tease him. I punish them and lecture them but it doesn't work. What shall I do to help this boy? Yours, Peter."

"Dear Peter: I really enjoy reading your letters. It breaks the monotony. I am not a wise woman, but I hope my simple solution to your student's problem may help you. Find an older popular student who is bright and willing to help to solve the problem. Ask the parents of the retarded student if they are willing to pay the popular student for his time. The student must have brunch, lunch, P.E. and an hour after school with the retarded student. Once the other students see that the popular student spends time with the retarded student, they will accept him. I hope this will help. Yours, Dorothy."

"Dear Dorothy: Thank you for showing an interest in my work. I tried your solution to the problem. The parents were delighted to hire the popular student and so far it is working fairly well. Time will tell. Dorothy, do you like to dance? Would you like to go dancing with me? Yours, Peter."

"Dear Peter: I wondered if you were going to ask me to go dancing with you. Next weekend there is a dance. Would you like to go to the dance? It isn't a date. I will meet you at the dance. If you like me we will dance all night, if not I will understand, and you can wander around. Yours, Dorothy."

"Dear Dorothy: I am looking forward to meeting you at the dance. Can you tell me, what you are planning to wear? I want to recognize you when I see you. I am counting the days until we meet. Yours, Peter."

"Dear Peter: I am also counting the days until we meet at the dance. This afternoon I went shopping for a new dress. The color of the dress is red. The skirt is short and the sleeves are short. The saleslady told me that the dress looks exquisite on me. Even though the dress was expensive, I bought it. I'm looking forward to seeing you. Yours, Dorothy."

Then the weekend arrived, and it was Saturday night. Peter went to the dance. He was early because he expected to meet Dorothy there. He was nervous. He looked like a high school kid. He walked around the dance hall, dreaming that he was dancing with Dorothy. He hoped that he didn't stutter. It was only eight O'clock. The dance had only just now started. There were more ladies than men. Several of the ladies were looking at him, but he wasn't interested. Then it was almost nine o'clock and Dorothy still wasn't at the dance. Peter bought a bottle of beer and was looking for Dorothy. He approached a few ladies dressed in red but they weren't Dorothy. Finally, it was twelve o'clock.

The dance ended and Dorothy hadn't shown up. Peter was angry. He called the police to find out if there was an accident and if Dorothy was hurt. They informed him that nobody got hurt that night.

The next morning Peter wrote a letter to Dorothy. He was angry. "Dear Dorothy: I went to the dance and I didn't see you. I made a fool of myself. I asked every women who wore a red dress if she was Dorothy. The women started teasing me and called me Dorothy. Please let me know what happened to you. Yours, Peter."

Dorothy replied to Peter: "Dear Peter: I was looking forward to meeting you. I had to work and my boss didn't let me out. You didn't give me your phone number and I was unable to call you. Please forgive me. Yours, Dorothy."

"Dear Dorothy: I hope that very soon we will be able to meet. Enclosed is my phone number. Please call me."

The next day Dorothy called Peter on the phone and said: "Hello, Peter. I hope you won't be angry when you meet me face to face. I have something I need to say to you, but I don't know how to start."

"Dorothy, get to the point," Peter said.

Dorothy was trembling. The words started to come out, faltered, started again, and she finally said, "I am ninety-two years old and I live in a convalescent home. I'm sorry for lying to you. I don't blame you if you don't want to meet me."

There was a period of silence as Peter digested this. Then he replied, "I will come to see you tomorrow after school."

Dorothy gave him the address, and hung up.

Peter still wanted to meet Dorothy. He sensed something special about her. The next day after school he bought a dozen red roses and went to the convalescent home to meet Dorothy. He was nervous because of her age. What condition would she be in? Could she even move at that age? Then he heard somebody playing the piano. He was flabbergasted when he discovered it was Dorothy. When she was finished playing he shyly introduced himself.

Dorothy and Peter sat talking on the piano bench long into the evening. They laughed, talked and ate. A friendship developed. It wasn't a romance, but each one helped fill a place of emptiness in the other. From then on, Peter came every weekend to see her.

32

The Roadrunner

Cecilia, for a middle-aged woman, was very well put together. Truly she was gorgeous. She wasn't working and she spent all her energy on her appearance. She was very well groomed, a platinum blond with bright green eyes, five feet tall and weighed 120 lbs.—and not even one wrinkle on her face. Her body had everything in just the right places, just the way I liked it. Her lips and fingernails were blood red. Looking at her made me feel young again, ready to start life with my one true love. We were a match from heaven; that's what I thought, and I wondered if I deserved such happiness.

What actually happened between Cecilia and me can best be illustrated by the mating rituals of the roadrunner. Every spring the male roadrunner looks around for the perfect mate. He starts his courtship by displaying himself. He is very picky and doesn't settle for just any old partner. He wants somebody to build a family, somebody healthy and strong, but also beautiful and loving. Somebody that wants to live the rest of her life with him. Somebody who is kind, sweet and turns his world upside-down.

Cecilia was the woman for me. When I talked to her on the phone she made me laugh. I couldn't wait to talk to her every night. We talked about the daily events, telling each other what we did during the day. At night I was dreaming about her, kissing the pillow and fantasizing that I was kissing Cecilia.

Once the roadrunner finds the perfect match, he will attract her by showing himself to her, by strutting around with a perfect posture in front of her, hoping she will respond to him.

I was all excited; finally I was going to have a date with Cecilia. I wore my best clothes: navy blue pants, powder blue shirt and I topped it off with a brand new white cashmere sweater. If clothes made the man I was as ready as the roadrunner.

I picked her up, took her for lunch and we walked on the beach together, the cool gentle waves lapping at our bare feet. She wore a white blouse and soft yellow pants. The blouse pushed forward just where it should, and I imagined the softness inside. I couldn't help notice that she walked in a way that made her hips turn with each step; beautifully, provocatively—at least to me.

I wanted to hold her hand, but when I took hold of it she withdrew it from mine. Why? Was she merely modest, or was she saying "hands off"? I didn't know, and was afraid to ask.

Just then she began to talk about her love of the ocean, and when she smiled the whole beach brightened. Her voice was musical and gay, not a care in the world. And here I was, walking beside her, a mature man, experienced, poised—and totally smitten by her...my poise gone, my wits gone...reduced to a blob of desirous jello, aching for the mere touch of her hand.

I knew it was true love because I was suffering. Is true love suffering or is it joy? I told myself to slow down, let her blossom, and then she will hold my hand, she will kiss me and she will love me.

If the roadrunner's mate doesn't pay any attention to him, he tries a new technique. He gathers some branches, twigs or sticks as if he is building a nest. If this doesn't work and she still doesn't pay any attention to him but keeps her nose in the air, then he uses his last tactic, which will either make or destroy him.

I try to win Cecilia by sending her a bouquet of flowers. I went to the flower shop and picked up the flowers. I picked up a dozen roses, each one a different color, starting with white and ending with dark red. Also there were tulips, daffodils and gladiolas. The bouquet that I arranged was a classic one, a breathtaking bouquet filled with love. There was a card saying "from your secret admirer," and my phone number. I never heard from her. I was disappointed, but like the roadrunner I didn't give up. The roadrunner's last tactic was to bring her some delicious offering, like a lizard or a grasshopper. The roadrunner will dig and pick up a worm, hunt a lizard, holding it in his beak, and drop the delicious food in front of her to let the smell drive her crazy. If she accepts it there is a match. If not, he will eat the food, and start searching for a new mate.

I invited Cecilia for dinner. Surprise! She accepted my dinner invitation. Not a word about the roses, nor was I about to mention them either. "Is six o'clock okay?" I asked. "Yes," she said, "that's fine. I'll be at your place at six."

I was the happiest man alive. Cecilia was coming for dinner!

A few narrow, dark thoughts intruded. Her actions were

strange...sending mixed messages. But I brushed them aside. She was coming! Nothing else mattered. She was coming!

I prepared a Spanish meal for her. I prepared a paella and gazpacho. I went early in the morning to the farmer's market to get the best products for the meal. I got rice, chicken, fish, crab, tomatoes. I spent the whole day cooking and dreaming how we will spend the evening together. The smell of the paella was overwhelming; onions, tomato, basil, garlic, sweet peppers, olive oil and saffron, swimming among the fresh shrimp, and chunks of tender sweet peppers. It had been simmering for two hours. I stirred it lovingly; each movement of the spoon was a caress to my Cecilia. This was going to be a paella to remember—worthy of my love.

I glanced around at my house. Everything was spotless. Fresh flowers. The table was set with the best linen cloth, the best china and silverware. I had a bottle of wine for dinner. Then I looked at my own clothes; perfect, not a spot or wrinkle. I could hardly wait. It was six o'clock and Cecilia wasn't here. I waited for her nervously. It was six fifteen and no Cecilia. It was six-thirty and still no Cecilia. I told myself maybe traffic was heavy.

Then it was seven o'clock. I called Cecilia by phone and there wasn't an answer. I knew Cecilia was on her way to see me. I put the food in the oven to heat so we could start the meal right away. Then it was eight o'clock. I worried about Cecilia. I called her and left her a message, that I was waiting for her. Now it was nine o'clock and I was hungry, so I started to eat by myself.

I called the police and they informed me that nobody had reported an accident. While I was eating I wondered where Cecilia was. I cried. I knew that men don't cry—they keep it inside. I was angry. I started to drink and the sweet wine tasted bitter in my mouth. I blamed myself, just like the roadrunner who brought his mate food and she rejected him. He stamped his feet and left her like a biting dog. Every bite I took of the food stuck in my throat. The rice, chicken and seafood was a battle at first. I couldn't swallow the food. The love turned to hate, and as I emptied .the plate my love disappeared.

I couldn't understand Cecilia. Why had she accepted the invitation and then let me down? I went to bed drunk.

Next morning I woke up ready to face the world. I went to work at the convalescent home, hoping I would meet a new person. I saw a new face, a smiling one. She asked me if we could have lunch. Just like the roadrunner, my search for a mate went on.

33

Sam, Mimi and Me

Ever since I lived alone, after the loss of my wife, my next door neighbor, Douglas, and his wife, Martha, had kept an eye on me. Every morning they called me and sometimes invited me to dinner. They watched my house when I went away. They picked up my mail and newspapers. Douglas was athletic and I often went to the gym with him. Martha was an excellent cook and she tried her food experiments out on me. I ate everything.

One day Douglas informed me that he and his wife had to leave town for two or three months. He didn't have anybody to take care of his dog, a cute little Shih-Tzu, so I decided to be my neighbor's dogsitter. I thought it would be better than sitting home, alone, feeling bad.

When I went to their home to see him, he was lying on the floor and was sleeping. "How hard would it be to take care of the dog?" I thought. He seemed very well behaved. His owners had done a very fine job of training him. The dog related well to strangers. He showed poise and grace, and appeared very confident to me. After all, he was a Shih-Tzu.

A Shih-Tzu is a breed of small, furry, toy dog that weighs twelve to fifteen pounds and its height is between ten and fifteen inches tall. Shih-Tzus originally came from China and Tibet. In Tibet they were kept in temples as sacred dogs.

The Shih-Tzu has a broad head and large, dark eyes. The dog's long, thick coat may be any color. My neighbor's Shih-Tzu was white, gray and black. His name was Sam.

When it was time for them to leave, Douglas and Martha left Sam with me. They gave me canned and dry food and told me to feed him once a day. Also, I got feeding and water bowls, his sleeping crate, a collar, leash and grooming supplies.

Sam seemed to feel very comfortable with me. While I was sitting on my favorite leather chair he jumped on me. He demanded to be pet-ted and groomed, and he loved to be massaged. At night he preferred to sleep on my bed, curled to my body, rather than sleeping in his crate.

I was afraid that when Douglas and Martha left Sam under my care, Sam would start whining. To preempt this I gave him a sock. He attacked the prey and quickly retreated to a corner of the room with it He played with it for hours, and the only time he let go of the sock was when I took him for a walk.

After I'd had Sam for two weeks, it was time to groom him and clip his nails. I had been brushing his hair every day and he enjoyed it very much; but bathing him and nail clipping was not my job—feeding him, cleaning his feces, walking with him and playing with him were all my jobs.

I didn't have to take Sam to a dog groomer, the groomer came to my house to take care of Sam. All of a sudden I had a strange feeling. The groomer seemed to be more concerned with breeding Sam than grooming him. He said that Sam would be an excellent stud. Sam had excellent pedigree papers. He was priceless.

The groomer asked me if I would like to breed Sam. He told me that he knew a female that was in heat and she was on the last few days of her cycle. If she wasn't pregnant this cycle they would have to wait another six months. I called Douglas and Martha and told them the news. They approved and were excited.

The groomer brought Mimi, a female Shih-Tzu, to my house. Sam was barking and protecting his territory. Mimi ignored him. She went to his food bowl and started eating Sam's food. Sam was ready to attack her; after all, she was eating his food and drinking his water. But he was not swayed by her attractiveness, even though she was a beautiful dog.

Sam would have nothing do with Mimi. He protected the sock that I had given him. I gave her a sock to play with. After a while they were both running around the house with the socks but they continued to ignore each other.

It was night and I went to bed. Both dogs jumped into bed with me. I slept in the middle of the bed and each one slept on opposite sides.

I thought that since this was the first day they met, maybe tomor-row they would mate.

The next day we got up late. The dogs felt cozy sleeping next to me. Sam was the first one to wake up. He licked me and I knew he had to go to the bathroom. Mimi had a hard time getting off the bed;

she was afraid to jump. I carried her outside and I thought maybe Sam would pay her some attention. I fed them, brushed them and took them for a walk. Sam pulled the leash and pulled Mimi. He wanted to show both of us that he was the master.

Meanwhile, Mimi was in heat. She raised her tail and assumed a mating stance. While we were walking, the male dogs in the neighborhood got excited and wanted to meet Mimi. Sam didn't care.

I was tired after walking outside with the dogs. I brought them home and I put them in the bedroom. I thought maybe in my bedroom, in a smaller area, they would get to know each other and eventually mate. I had only a few hours left while Mimi was in heat; it would be another six months before Mimi would be in heat again.

They both were lying on opposite sides of the room. Sam wasn't barking, and Mimi was slyly coming closer to Sam. I took them to the bathroom which was an even smaller room. Sam urinated on the floor to mark his territory. Mimi was smelling the urine and came closer to Sam. I put a blanket in the bathroom tub and put the two dogs in the tub. I closed the door and let them have privacy for mating.

A few hours later I saw them lying next to each other. I took them out of the bathroom and let them walk outside in the backyard. They were walking like lovers. Sam had a gleam in his eyes. Mimi looked happy and she was licking Sam. They paid no attention to me.

A few days later, Douglas and Martha returned home. I thought that they would have a hard time getting Sam back, but Sam was a traitor. Whoever fed him, petted him and groomed him was his master of the moment. In order to win Sam back they gave him some bacon.

Three months after Sam met Mimi, she gave birth to seven puppies. Mimi was not a young dog. I was surprised that she had given birth to seven puppies. There were four girls and three boys.

I was also surprised and saddened to find out that there was some kind of complication, and Mimi had died shortly after delivering the seven puppies.

Mimi wasn't buried in a cemetery. She was wrapped in a black bag and thrown into a dumpster. Everybody forgot about her.

This lovely little dog had given birth to a total of fourteen puppies in her lifetime. She had earned her keep. The owner sold the puppies and never even mentioned Mimi.

I wondered if Sam remembered her. A few weeks after the puppies were born, I got permission from Douglas and Martha to take Sam to the pet store to see his litter. When we arrived and I placed Sam with the puppies, he didn't take any notice of them; he only wanted a biscuit bone as a treat. The puppies licked him and he ran away from them.

Several months passed and one day I saw Sam in the neighborhood. I thought we were good friends, but every time I approached Sam he bared his teeth at me and made an aggressive growling sound as if he was ready to attack me. I brought him a dog biscuit and he suddenly became friendly.

I wondered if it had been worthwhile to take care of him. I decided that, yes, indeed, it had been. I had done my neighbors a favor. Mimi was gone, but there were seven new puppies ready to have fun and explore the world. I had recently lost my wife, and Sam had kept me occupied during the most difficult days when I wished that I had been taken along with her.

When I was down, Sam had lifted me up. Now when he growled at me, I was able to growl back at him.

And the healing continued.

34

The Ten Children

After I lost my wife to cancer, I was alone with time on my hands and I decided to come to the convalescent home every day, to eat with the residents, push their wheelchairs, talk to them and just be with them. Associating with the elders gave me pleasure and helped with healing my own grief, plus volunteering at the convalescent home was paying back society for taking good care of my mother-in-law.

Maria had been my mother-in-law's nurse aide. Now I was surprised to find her in the convalescent home as a resident instead of an employee.

Maria was an elderly woman. When I had first met her she was seventy years old and worked at the convalescent home. She had been working in the kitchen, cooking, and in the dining room, feeding the residents. She had fed my mother-in-law when Anna hadn't been able to feed herself.

Maria was excellent. Anna wouldn't eat for me because I was impa-

tient with her. Also, she didn't want me to see her in her present con-
dition-she wanted me to remember her strong and healthy. But for
Maria, she ate. Maria was patient with her and was always joking and
telling her stories. Maria often told her, "Don't give up, Anna."

Maria was a small but strong woman. She had dark skin, straight
black hair that smelled good, and large, dark eyes. She told me that she
had come across the border from Mexico with her husband to work as
a farm laborer. She had worked very hard on the farm, picking fruit and
vegetables. Every year she was blessed with a child. She'd had ten girls.
Maria told me she, herself, was named after the Virgin Mary. And in
turn, she named each of her daughters Maria: Maria Blanca, Maria
Dolores, etc. She'd had her girls baptized and the priest knew the first
name of each girl—*Maria.*

Maria remembered that she had never gone to school, and she
made sure that all her daughters graduated from high school. Maria
Blanca was the oldest daughter, and Maria felt that if she did well in
school, the others would follow her example. They did, and some of
them became nurses and teachers. Feeding and dressing her ten daughters, and taking care of their health, had been a difficult job for Maria—
her husband never seemed to have time to help.

After living on a farm for fifteen years, Maria's family had moved to
a small town where they had bought a house. It was directly across
from the convalescent home. Maria had worked at the convalescent
home for fifty years!

Maria loved cats. When her girls left home and her husband died,
she replaced them with cats. She had cats everywhere. There were cats
on the refrigerator, on the bed, and on tables and chairs.

Then, when she was quite old, Maria was unable to take care of
herself and she became a resident at the same convalescent home

where she had worked for so many years. Even without her cats, Maria was a happy person. She loved to laugh. Everything made her happy.

When Maria was employed by the convalescent home she had enjoyed working in the kitchen. She loved to make sandwiches. At lunch time the residents ate their main meal: chicken, beef stew, etc., but at night they ate soup and sandwiches. Maria would cut the bread into little triangles. She would spread mustard or mayonnaise on the bread and add corned beef, roast beef, baloney and cheese. Now she told me she had earned the right to be served, herself, and to eat somebody else's sandwiches.

When I first saw her as a resident, she recognized me right away and she said, "I guess you can't run away from this place, Alex."

"No, Maria, nobody can run away from this place. How are your children and grandchildren?"

Maria looked at me sadly and said, "I thought that at least one of my daughters would take care of me, just like I cared for my mother and mother-in-law."

"Maria," I said, "looking at you old and sick breaks my heart."

"Oh, Alex, it's not so bad. This is my whole world. Some of the patients I took care of years ago are still alive and I enjoy their company."

"What do you do all day?"

"Alex, for the first time in my life I am doing some things for myself. Laura is teaching me to read and write. I hope that when my grandchildren come to visit me I will be able to read to them." Maria looked sad, and continued, "My daughters call me once a week but I see the grandchildren only rarely."

I told her, "I am sorry that you don't see your grandchildren more often, but, as you said, at least now you can take time for yourself. And besides, now you are getting an education."

Maria was still reflecting on the past, and she replied, "You know, Alex, it wasn't easy to get the job I had. Nothing was easy, with ten girls to raise. When I first got the job here, I put on a new, navy blue uniform, I went to the kitchen right away, and started cutting vegetables and making soup. I lasted fifty years at the same job."

Old and tired as she looked, there was an inner beauty about Maria. Maybe it was the beauty that comes from a life spent taking care of others. I looked at her and thought, "If a mother can raise ten children, why can't ten children take care of one parent?"

35

Friendship

After my wife died I decided that in addition to volunteering at the convalescent home, I was going to volunteer at the local high-school. I had an important message to share with the students about friendship. I hoped to interest the students in volunteering at the convalescent home and learning the value of having an older person as a friend.

I asked them: "What is friendship?" Here are some of their actual responses, which I have neither made up nor altered.

A seventeen-year-old male student who was very serious and precise and to the point wrote: "Friendship is a priceless gift, that you treasure and share."

A fourteen-year-old girl wrote this. She was short, had medium hair, blackish brownish eyes, impatient and very talkative. "Friendship means to me support and kindness. Friends mean helping, sharing, caring and understanding. Friendship is listening to one's problems and being there in a time of need. Friendship is not criticizing and insulting but supporting and complimenting. It means to help instead of ignore and to defend instead of insult."

A fifteen-year-old girl who loved to play soccer and had dirty blond hair and blue eyes, was too shy to tell me about friendship, but she wasn't afraid to write about it. This is what she wrote: "Friendship is one of the most important things in life. If you have no friends, you have nothing. Friends provide love that can help you get through any obstacle in life. Friends are more important than anything. They are an extension of your family. So the more you have, the better off you are."

A seventeen-year-old Hispanic girl told me that she had no idea what she would do when she grew up and she hated it when people asked her about it. She wrote this little essay: "Friendship is a single soul dwelling in two bodies. Life is nothing without friendship. The only way to have a friend is to be one. Shared joy is double joy, shared sorrow is half sorrow. The essence of friendship is not getting, but sharing. A life without a friend is a life without a sun.

"Wear a smile and have friends; wear a scowl and have wrinkles. Whoever you are it is your own friends who make your world. A friend is one who knows all about you and likes you anyway. Hold a true friend with both your hands. Flowers of true friendship never fade.

"Your wealth is where your friends are. True friendship comes when silence between two people is comfort. The best mirror is an old friend."

A crew-cut boy student who loves to play basketball and write poetry wrote this: "Friendship doesn't have any specific meaning, but only feeling can say what friendship is all about. From my experience, I can say that friendship is love, caring, understanding, forgiving and many other positive things that friends (people) like to share with one another. Friendship is not a word that can be defined with words, it can only be shown with action."

After they had written about friendship, I asked the students if I could tell them a story. They were very excited about what I had to say. This is what I told them.

At the age of twelve, my wife, Margaret, emigrated from Australia to the United States. She started school and she was very nervous. Slowly, she started to make some friends. There was a set of twins that she liked, Daisy and Dana. They were identical twins. Margaret was the only one that could tell them apart.

The twins' parents were divorced. Their mother, with whom they lived, was a nurse and she raised the girls by herself. When Margaret came home from school, she had a loving mother waiting for her. Her mother prepared a snack for her and asked her about her day at school, then she prepared a snack for her before Margaret did her homework.

The twins, on the other hand, came home to an empty house. Their mother was at work. They had to make their own snack, clean the house, wash their clothes and make supper.

Margaret became their friend. She invited them to come to her house to do their homework. Margaret's mother treated them just like her own daughter. She made them snacks and she went shopping with them. Margaret felt good because Daisy and Dana were her closest friends.

Once Margaret became friends with the twins she was able to make many more friends, but the twins were special. The three of them made a pact: "One for all and all for one."

The girls grew. They graduated from middle school and then from high school. Then they faced the world. Daisy and Dana went to a vocational school and they became secretaries. Margaret went to college and became a social worker. They were still close friends. They spent every weekend together.

Dana was the first one to get married and she moved far away. Daisy, after losing her twin sister, became an even closer friend to Margaret. After work they went everywhere together. They double dated, went shopping and went on vacation together. Then Daisy got married, but didn't forget her friend. Margaret married me, and the four of us-Margaret, me, Daisy and her husband-were inseparable. We dined, we danced, we worked together. We were young and very happy.

Margaret and I bought our house in the same neighborhood as Daisy's house. Our house was only a few blocks away. Since the houses were new, we helped each other decorate and landscape them. A few years later we were blessed with two children: a girl and a boy. Daisy had two girls the same age as our children. We raised our children together, they went to the same school and all four became good friends. We watched them grow; they played sports and practiced music together. We took vacations together, we went to church together; we were of the same religion.. We celebrated birthdays and holidays together.

Then, all of a sudden Daisy divorced her husband and we didn't see her or her children for several years because she left town without a forwarding address. Several months later, Daisy came back with her new husband.

Margaret and I, and our son and daughter, thought we could all be friends again. After all, Daisy had been my wife's best friend. "One for all and all for one," was their motto.

But we noticed that Daisy's new husband seemed to resent us. We reminded him of a past in which he'd had no part, and he pressured Daisy to break up with her old friends. Margaret reminded Daisy that their friendship was a bond between them, and Daisy shouldn't throw away what they'd had for thirty years. But Daisy chose her husband's feelings, and broke up with us.

One day Margaret invited Daisy for lunch at a restaurant and, surprisingly, Daisy accepted. Margaret pleaded with her, "Daisy, you and your sister were my first friends. I was a stranger in this place, and you made me welcome." Daisy couldn't face Margaret. She looked away and replied," We outgrew each other. I couldn't tell you on the phone how I felt, and that's why I accepted your invitation for lunch. Please don't call me again."

Margaret was crying. "What did I do that I deserve this treatment?"

They ordered food but they couldn't eat. There was terrible tension in the air.

Daisy said, "Aren't you being too hysterical? Didn't we just out grow each other?"

Margaret replied, "You were my bridesmaid, you were my classmate, you were my best friend. I was your friend when you divorced your husband. When you were sad I made you feel happy. Friendship is very important to me. I will fight for our friendship."

But Daisy was not impressed. She laughed and said, "I'm looking for new friends. I'm starting a new life and I want to forget the past. I'm sorry, but I don't want anything to do with you."

Margaret grabbed the napkin and dried her eyes. She paid the bill and before she left she said, "If you are trying to forget the past and your ex-husband, you can't. Just look at your daughters and they will remind you of the past. A friend does not betray you. Friendship is a gift. You may not want anything to do with me, but don't forget me."

Margaret drove home. She was crying all the way home. I tried to cheer her up. I called Daisy and pleaded with her not to end the friendship. I told her, "Friendship is a large part of our life. If we had to go through life without any friends then there would be no reason to stay alive."

Daisy mocked me. She told me, "Friendship to me means my husband, and he is all I care about. He wants me to forget my past before him." And that was the last time we spoke to her.

Years passed; out of sight out of mind. We had pretty much forgotten about Daisy and her family. We knew that our children and theirs had gone to college. Our kids left the house and had their own life. We were left all alone. From time to time we talked about getting in touch with Daisy and her husband, but never tried again.

Then my wife became sick. At first I couldn't say the name of the disease. We called it the terrible "C." Now I can say it: Cancer.

My wife lasted only nine months after she had been diagnosed with the disease. Somehow, Daisy found out that my wife was sick one month before she died. She mailed her a card that said: "Wishing you pleasant days, restful nights and a speedy recovery. Daisy."

There wasn't a return address or a phone number on the card.

I asked my wife if she wanted me to get in touch with Daisy. I knew where she lived. I could call the telephone operator and get her telephone number. My wife took the card, crumbled it and threw it into the garbage can.

Two weeks before my wife died, a mutual friend of ours told Daisy that Margaret was dying. Daisy replied, "So what do you want me to do about it?"

Our friend told her "Aren't you her friend?"

Daisy replied, "That was a long time ago."

><>-O-<><

After I finished the story, I asked the students what they felt about it. One of my students wrote this about friendship.

"Friendship is like the wind in a baby's lungs that falls closely to the mountain side. A friend you can lean on, and smell the breath of your soul in their heart. A note to a friend: 'I've never been very smart, but I connect you to your shadow.'

"Only a drop of wine and the sky's jealousy can break true friends apart. The syncopated admiration of a river can only begin to explain the love and beauty between genuine friends."

36

The Bus Ride

After my wife died I was very restless. One day, after spending part
of the morning and the afternoon in the convalescent home volunteering my services, I decided to take the bus downtown. At the bus stop
there were high school kids yelling at each other, laughing and pushing each other. It took a long time for all of them to get on, and the
bus was getting full.

The students were all excited. Their high school team was in the
basketball finals. If they won this game they would be eligible to play
in the state championships. All I heard was "Jaime was great." And
"Eduardo was even better." The girls were thrilled about Jaime. "He is
sooooo good looking," one said.

"Does he have a girlfriend?" another one said.

"Who cares if he has a girlfriend? The only thing important is that
we win the game," said the third girl.

They were shouting, they were yelling with excitement and showing each other that they had tickets for the basketball game. All of a
sudden I overheard something that caught my attention. One of the
kids told his friends that he wasn't going to the game. He had a five-
piece band and they would be practicing at his house. Everybody was
surprised that his parents allowed him to play the instruments at his
home. He informed them that they found termites in his house. Once
he started playing the instruments and using the amplifier, the termites
left the house. They couldn't stand the vibration and the loudspeakers.
That's why his father let the band practice in the house.

The students had now all boarded the full bus. Then I saw her get
on. The most beautiful woman I had ever seen.

My heart started to pound. She was absolutely gorgeous. She was
tall with dark, olive skin and black hair. She looked like a Greek god-
dess. She wore golden loop earnings.

I was looking at her and thinking, "What a beautiful view." I was watching her but I didn't want to be caught. Her eyes were brown, dark brown, the color of the earth soil. They looked like chocolate.

Then I saw her look at me. She was standing in the middle of the bus, holding a pole. I was sitting at the front of the bus. If I was a gentleman I would offer her my seat, but I was too shy. I wished I was one of the high school kids going to the basketball game. I could invite her to the game. We would sit on the same bench, holding hands, maybe sharing the same drink. After the game we would celebrate our team's victory by going to a dance. The kid's band, the one I overheard him talking about at the bus stop, would play at the dance. We would dance cheek to cheek.

But I was shy. I am still shy.

The high school kids left and the bus was suddenly half empty. My imagined date had a girlfriend and they both sat in the middle of the bus. I glanced at her. She glanced back at me but our eyes never met. She looked stunning with her black shining hair. The wind in the bus blew her hair and I had a good look at her without being caught. She opened her mouth and had perfect white teeth. I wondered if they were real, and thought about my own looks. I was sixty years old and she was probably forty. But I looked young for my age. I had a full head of dark hair and I was slim because I worked out every day at the gym. I enjoyed swimming and exercising.

She and I were playing a silly game. We were playing hide and seek or cat and mouse with our eyes. I gave her what I thought was a meaningful glance. Her mouth was small. I wondered if she was a good kisser. I thought, "Maybe I should approach her, sit closer to her," since there were several empty seats in front of her. I wanted to hear her voice, laughing or talking. But I was afraid.

She was tapping her watch. She was lifting her arm to hear the watch and looked at the time. This was my chance! I could tell her the time and start a conversation with her. She raised her eyebrows and looked helpless. She was laughing coquettishly and getting quite a lot of attention on the bus. She wore a white blouse and a long, black skirt, both fitted seductively and tightly on her body. I hoped that one of the buttons would pop to give me a better view. I felt like a dirty old man.

By this time the bus was almost empty, with only a few passengers left. I could ask her if she would join me for a cup of coffee. I pretended I wasn't looking at her. It was hurtful that we were so close and yet so far away. This was my chance. I didn't want to be alone any more, sleeping alone, getting up alone, eating alone, having only one toothbrush when before there were two.

We could have breakfast, lunch or dinner together. I told myself "Go, go, go talk to her." I had a strange feeling she wanted to talk to me. "Talk to her—she isn't going to bite you," I thought.

I was ready but I lost my voice; the words couldn't come out. But my imagination raced on. She could cook for me, live with me, share everything I had, could sleep with me and could make love to me.

I was so preoccupied with my thoughts of her that I didn't realize she had left the bus.

➤⊢⬦➤⬦O⬦⬧⊢⬦

I imagined several ways that our story might end. In the first version, I jumped out of the bus when she got off and I followed her. I introduced myself and she seemed pleased to meet me. We walked to a grocery store. There we got two steaks, two potatoes for baking, a bottle of wine, fixings for a salad and strawberries. While choosing the strawberries she would steal one or two and feed them to me. Maybe I would steal a few grapes and feed her. The sweetness of the fruit would make us love each other.

In the next version I followed her and almost caught up with her, but she was faster than me, being younger and lighter. I sat down on a bench and was angry at myself for losing her. Then, suddenly I saw her. I approached her. She turned around and it wasn't her–only someone wearing the same clothes.

In the third version we both left the bus at the same time. I approached her and asked if she would like to have a cup of coffee with me. But she ran to a nearby policeman and told him, "Officer, this man is stalking me."

In the final version, I was on the bus and didn't realize she had left. I wasn't worried because I would see her tomorrow at the bus stop. The next day I drove to the bus stop where she had gotten on but I didn't see her. For a week I didn't see her. Then I decided to take the bus, myself. I dressed to kill: sharp fitting Levi slacks, green sweater and tennis shoes. I asked the bus driver if he had seen her. The bus driver replied, "Didn't you read the paper?" "No, I didn't," I said. He informed me that some factories had closed, and she had worked in one of the factories. The high-school kids were all laughing at me. I told them to shut up. I guess I lost her. Two years later a mutual friend introduced us—the very same woman—and six months later we were married. On our wedding day I asked her if she remembered when we had first seen each other. She told me, "Yes." She wondered why I didn't have the courage to approach her. I lied. I told her, "I wasn't ready. I was mourning my wife."

She replied, "We wasted two and a half precious years of our lives until we found each other again."

>-+◆>-O-<◆+-<

But the truth is, I was shy. And I never saw her again.

37

The Group

One day I saw an ad in the local newspaper.

Grief: a normal process of sharing needs and feelings.
Rain or shine meets every Thursday, 6-7:30 p.m.
For 52 weeks a year at xxxxxxxxx hospital.
$3.00 per session.

Since I was depressed and I couldn't stand staying at home alone, I decided to give them a chance and go to a meeting. All the people would be in the same boat as I was, and therefore we could relate to each other. Maybe after the meeting I could go to dinner with some of the members at a local restaurant.

I arrived early in order to meet the social worker. She was an older woman almost my age, dressed nicely in a navy blue, silk, two-piece suite, navy blue shoes, a white blouse, a red scarf and a navy blue purse. She had the nicest smile. She had blonde curly hair, brown eyes and her voice was low and sweet. I felt comfortable being with her, as though I could tell her all my intimate secrets. Even though I just met her I felt I had known her for years.

Maybe I could tell her that I lost my wife after being married for thirty two years. I could tell her that I still cry at night when I am alone in bed. I could tell her that I am afraid to be alone, that I am shaking so hard that I think that I am having a heart attack. But in the morning when the sun is up, everything is all right and I am still alive.

I could tell her that I wonder what is wrong with me. I have a warm, safe place to live in, a clean bed to sleep on, good food to eat, clean clothes to wear and a hot shower...but that I have been scared and worried since I lost my wife.

But I didn't say any of these things; the rest of the group was arriving.

We were a group of twelve people, the social worker and eleven of us. There were four men, including me, and seven women. It seems to me that those programs appeal more to women than men. Men are afraid to cry in public, and are embarrassed talking in groups about personal matters.

We started introducing ourselves and mentioning what we did last week, as a way of beginning lightly. Then we started telling why we were there. Mostly, the others were there to try to learn how to cope with losing a loved one. The first person to speak was a woman who had lost her husband seven months ago. She told us that she couldn't get rid of her husband's clothes. "It's like he is on a business trip, and he'll be home soon," she told us. I felt the same way when my wife died. I couldn't get rid of her clothes, even though she had asked me to give them to the convalescent home. As long as I had her clothes in the house I felt she was coming back.

There was an older man in his eighties, who had lost his wife three years ago, and the only family he had was this support group. He invited the whole group to dinner on his wife's birthday. He wanted to share his cooking ability and also didn't want to be alone on his wife's birthday. I didn't know him well so I declined. I hoped that he didn't think that I was a snob.

The next person was a woman who had recently lost her son. He had been shot by accident. The bullet had penetrated his heart and he died on the spot. She was crying, and I felt sympathy for her. Our children are supposed to bury us, we aren't supposed to bury our children.

There was also a daughter and mother who had lost their father and husband. The daughter seemed to take it harder than her mother. She wanted to erect a plaque in memory of her father in the public library, but her mother was against it. The daughter also wanted to raise money for a scholarship in memory of her father, but again her mother was against it. Mother and daughter didn't get along very well. They both were strong and stubborn women.

The mother wasn't crying but the daughter was. The mother was angry that her husband had left her. He had gone fishing, gotten drunk and had fallen off the boat and was drowned. The daughter told us that her mother was a good mother and an excellent wife. Her entire world was her five children and her husband. She didn't work; she was a housewife. She had never gone beyond high school. Her whole life revolved around her husband, children, church and community.

Some of the members brought cookies and we passed them around. The room was small, with only fifteen chairs, a table with a water pitcher, and a few paper cups and tissues. It was cozy.

Fortunately, there were only twelve people in the room, otherwise we would have been like sardines in a can.

We were all seated in our chairs except one lady. She was a curly-headed blond who couldn't sit still and kept pacing back and forth. She wore Levi slacks, a Levi shirt and leather boots. She opened her purse and showed us a pair of small, silver owl candelabras. They were hand-made. They looked beautiful. It was her turn to tell us about herself. She told about losing her husband to cancer. Before he died he left her a letter telling her how much he loved her. It is very important that a loved one leaves, besides pleasant memories, a letter to the one he is leaving behind. This letter is a refresher, a foundation for the living one. When you are down and feeling low, this letter will lift you up. The blond woman told us she had gone to their bank safety deposit box and had found the letter and the candelabras. To celebrate this she went to her favorite restaurant for dinner, and she lit the candles using those candelabras. She felt that her husband had joined her. The waiter knew her and her husband. He brought her two dinners and charged her only for one.

Then it was my turn, and I introduced myself and I told them I had lost my wife to cancer, and how hard it had been for me since then. There were a couple of moments that I choked up and couldn't talk, but I got through it.

The session was coming to an end. There was an older woman dressed in black shoes, black socks, black slacks, black sweater and black cap. She wasn't wearing any makeup and she was crying. She told us that nobody had suffered as much as she had. "In the same year I lost two loved ones," she said. I felt sorry for her and I was curious to find out who she had lost. I asked the group and they answered me in unison, "Don't you know?" I told them that it was my first visit. I asked her if she lost her husband. The woman in black replied that he was well and healthy.

"Did you lose your children?"

"No."

"Did you lose your parents, brothers, sisters, or in-laws?"

"No, but my tragedy is greater than any of you. In one year I lost my two great loves—my dog and my cat. I cannot describe the pain."

I tried to calm her by telling her that time will heal, and then she would be able to replace them. She asked me if I could replace my children. I told her no. I asked her if she had any other pets. She said that she had eight dogs and four cats. She then let the group know that she had cremated her pets and was going to spread the ashes in her backyard where she planted azaleas.

The session ended and we all hugged each other and said we would see each other next week. The social worker stopped me and gave me some papers to fill out: my name, age, address, phone number and members of my family. I asked her if there was any support groups for those who have lost their pets. She told me that the woman didn't feel comfortable in any other group; she loves our group.

I wondered aloud about the woman in black. If she still had twelve pets left, I said, she would probably be in the group for a very long time.

The social worker, whom I had thought to be so nice, apparently didn't take kindly to my comment. She looked at me and said, in a cold, emotionless voice, that she thought I would be better served by joining a different grief group.

I asked myself what was the purpose of going to the support group. First, I wanted to meet new people who were in the same boat as I. Second, I wanted to see how people who lost a loved one coped, and third, I wanted to have dinner with some of the people of the group.

But instead, the old man dressed in a suit, tie and vest invited me to come to his house. He whispered to me, "Please come to my house and help celebrate my wife's birthday." His eyes that had seen so much of the world were now begging. He said, "I only live a few blocks from here. Please come join us for dinner." I couldn't say no to his face, but I didn't show up.

The next person I saw, I sneered at. How stupid she was. She was going to a restaurant and eating by herself, pretending that her husband was with her.

I was so critical of these people because they were me. I didn't want to be part of them—I wanted my wife back!

At the same time, I was terribly angry at my wife who had left me. Why did she have to do that? I wanted her to be alive so we could eat together in a restaurant under a candelabras light. I wanted to get away to a romantic place and walk with her, holding hands tenderly.

But she was gone.

I went home, scolding myself for being such a snob. I was depressed when I left the house and I was depressed when I came back.

Only time will heal my sorrow.

38

The End

One of the hardest words to say in the English language or any other language is "cancer." It is a strange cry in the night that says you are probably going to die. When my wife was diagnosed with the disease I thought if I didn't mention it, or talk about it, it would go away.

To my great and terrible disappointment, it didn't. My wife was operated on, had chemotherapy, radiation, and after nine months she died.

Cancer is a killer. It is a terrorist. You never know where or when it will attack you next. It hides out in the body, then suddenly takes you hostage. Tumors appear and you are afraid they will hurt you and kill you. You are happy if you win a battle, but you haven't won the war. You use chemotherapy to destroy the cancer cells. But those cancer terrorists decide to attack a new organ and perhaps, finally, you get weak and give up.

Whatever cancer cells we weren't able to remove with surgery we treated with radiation, but it didn't do any good. I negotiated with God, I asked him to give my wife five more years, but Margaret said, "God gave me fifty-three wonderful years. I don't ask him for more."

Then I negotiated with God for four years, three years, two, even for one year. She died after nine months of terrible pain.

When Margaret took her third chemotherapy treatment she knew she would lose all her hair. It fell like hail. Clumps of hair fell when she washed it or combed it. It was a frightening sight. Sophia, our daughter, was mad at her mother because she went with a friend to buy a wig. Sophia asked, "Why didn't you take me with you to buy the wig?"

Margaret answered, "I didn't want to cause you pain when you saw me trying on wigs." Then she turned to me and asked, "Would you like to live with a blond or a redhead?" I told her it's not the outside that I am looking at, but the inside, and that's what I'll always love.

I didn't peek when I saw her bald. I was mad at myself because I covered my eyes when I entered the room. She told me, "Don't be afraid. It is me, Margaret, and I love you very much."

I wanted to stay out of the room. I didn't want to see her crying. I was crying. Was her disease a tragedy or a curse? She told me, "Don't worry. Soon my hair will grow back." She tried to convince me, to promise me that everything would be okay. I sat next to her, held her hand and told her not to talk too much. She told me that she had a lot of things to tell me. I only asked her to hug and kiss me.

Sophia asked her mother if it was okay if she shaved her head to show sympathy. "Dad and Ben will, too!" she added.

Margaret said, "No, please don't. I don't want to be reminded." As is sometimes the case, she and Sophia were becoming more friendly because of Margaret's illness. At least something good came from something so terrible.

The next day Sophia went for a haircut, but she didn't cut all her hair as she had first offered. Instead, she brought a tin can and asked the beautician if she would donate the cost of the haircut to the American Cancer Society. The beautician agreed, and the rest of the clients did the same.

While the beautician was fixing Sophia's hair, Sophia was daydreaming. She was visualizing that the town of 5,000 residents all had their heads shaved and donated the money to the cancer society in support of Margaret, her mother.

Sophia remembered that when she was at school she had heard a dynamic speaker raising money for the cancer society. At that time Sophia was happy to leave her regular class to go to the auditorium so she could be with her friends. She didn't pay attention to the speaker, and by the end of the speech they passed some boxes to collect money for the cancer society. She dropped a few coins into the box and left for home without thinking about this event.

Now that her mother was sick with cancer she remembered the speaker. She was an older woman in her seventies. She had told the students that she had cancer and had addressed them directly: "Look at me. I am your neighbor. You see me now. Would you like to see me alive next week? Can you spare your lunch money or your date money to donate to the cancer society? I hope that we will find a cure for my disease."

The speaker was tall and slim; she looked like a model. She didn't look sick, even though she had breast cancer. She was a wife, a mother and a grandmother. She only asked to live for a few more months until they would find a cure for her.

Back at the hair salon, Sophia now sat and was crying, and she also asked for a few more months for her mother to live until they would find a cure for her. Now, having her mother struck with the disease, Sophia understood what the speaker had been talking about in her class so long ago. She blamed herself that she hadn't done anything for the cancer society before. If she had done something earlier, perhaps they could have found a cure for her mother.

Sophia thought about what she could have done. She could have organized walks and gotten sponsors. She could have baked and sold cookies for the cancer society. Her friends could wash cars for a good cause.

She remembered the first time she heard the word cancer. It was when she was in the second grade. Her next door neighbor's uncle had died of cancer. The next door neighbor held a garage sale and the money they raised they donated to the cancer society.

Her friend donated her old clothes and toys. Sophia only had enough money to buy one item. She had wanted two things: a doll and a straw purse. Finally, she settled for the doll. Now she blamed herself that she hadn't participated further in the garage sale. She could have donated some of her old clothes and toys to help raise money for cancer.

Cancer is a killer. You block the word cancer and only when a loved one is hit with the disease do you start to do something about it.

My wife was on trial. I wonder what crime she committed. The prosecutor attacked her without remorse. The defense attorney defended her and fought for her. The defense attorney was the doctor, and he operated on her, gave her chemotherapy and radiation therapy, while the prosecutor was the cancer. The decision went to the jury and the verdict was in. Finally, after nine months, the prosecutor won. The cancer killed her.

A year after my wife died, my daughter Sophia told me, "Dad, I decided to raise money for cancer. I'm willing to participate, both physically and mentally. There is a 60-mile walk for cancer."

I replied, "Sophia, I will support you. Walking sixty miles is a big job. Are you really willing to take the challenge?"

Sophia replied, "Dad, I'm only going to walk twenty miles a day. There will be five thousand men and women who will walk with me. I know that Mom will watch me."

"Sophia, we will all support you, monetarily and emotionally."

My daughter started practicing walking five miles every day. Also she raised two thousand dollars for cancer research. The day arrived when she started walking. The temperature early in the morning was seventy degrees Fahrenheit and at lunch time it reached ninety degrees. My daughter was sweating, and she told me, "Mom is watching me. Just like she taught me to sit, to crawl, to walk and to run, she is now watching me walking for this cause."

Sophia accomplished her mission and told me, "Mom was there. When I was hot, she sent a breeze to cool me. When I was stiff and sore, she healed me. Just thinking about her made the journey easier for me."

39

The Pulse

I have written a book called *The Forgotten People: People Without Faces*. After completing the book and sending it to the publisher, I asked myself the following question: What have I learned from the experience of my wife's illness and death?

When my wife was diagnosed with cancer I was shocked and didn't believe it. How could it be? My wife was always the strongest one. She always made decisions for us; where we lived, where the children went to school, what car we drove. When she informed me that she was sick. I told her it was okay, I would take care of her, but I didn't know how to start taking care of her.

At first I tried to ignore the sickness, believing it would go away. I believed that we didn't invite the sickness and it should have the courtesy to go away! We cut the tumor, we burned it and we poisoned it, but it didn't go away.

I learned through her ordeal to be strong; and watching her suffering gave me courage to face the world.

Another question I asked myself: What have I learned from having to live alone?

I learned to be tolerant and patient. In our marriage she was the strong one. Suddenly we switched roles. I became the strong one and she completely leaned on me. I had a hard time making the bed, going grocery shopping and cleaning the house. My wife had paid the bills and balanced the checkbook, and believe it or not I didn't know how to do it. Now, all alone, I learned to do it while keeping a job and taking care of the house.

Another question I asked myself: What have I learned from my experiences at the convalescent home?

Thanks to modern medicine we are living longer, but I wonder if we are really living better. Nobody wants to die; we all look for a miracle. Visiting the convalescent home and volunteering taught me a lesson. Those old people have a lot to offer the next generation. They can teach the youth. There are many youths that live with single parents, who go home after school to an empty house. Instead of that, like the boy, Oscar, in my book, they can visit the old people.

Each one needs the other. One hand needs the other hand and both hands can wash the face.

Another question I asked myself: How am I a different person from the man I was before all of this happened?

After being married for thirty-two years to the same woman, we became as one. At first we were two people and then we melted as one. We started to look alike, talk alike and think alike. When she died I thought the world ended for me.

I heard a silly story that I want to share with you.

The Pulse

Once upon a time there was a man who didn't have a pulse. If you don't have a pulse you don't have a heart. If you don't have a heart you don't have blood. If you don't have a pulse, a heart and blood, you are supposed to be dead. But this man was alive and healthy.

He was tall and handsome. He was slim and athletic. He worked out at the gym for hours. Since he didn't have a pulse he was never breathless. He was happy. He didn't worry about anything. He knew that half of the things that we worry about never come true; that we usually worry for nothing.

The man without a pulse never let anything aggravate him. His wife, on the other hand, worried all the time. She was a nurse and she would nag him forever. She would worry about day-to-day living. On the other hand, he never worried and he was happy.

His wife nagged him about his pulse. She couldn't find his pulse. She used a stethoscope and couldn't hear his heart. She cut him and he didn't bleed. She took him to a doctor and the doctor couldn't find his heart.

The doctor told him, "You don't have a heart, and I wonder how you are alive."

The man replied, "But I am alive. What should I do?"

The doctor replied, "Go to another country; maybe they can find your heart."

So the man traveled all over the world but nobody could help him. Then he found out that there was a wise man who might be able to help him to find his pulse. The wise man was old. He had white hair, a white mustache and a white beard. He had light blue eyes. He was all wrinkled, short and fat. He had a friendly face and when he talked to you, you felt good about yourself.

The man without a pulse approached the wise man and said, "Hello."

The wise man said, "Hello, what can I do for you?"

He said, "I am the man without a pulse. Can you help me find my pulse?"

The wise man gleamed. All his life he was trying to be calm, relaxed and he wanted to lose his pulse because once he lost his pulse he would reach *utopia*. So he was happy to greet the man. He told him, "All my life I have been looking for somebody like you. If you teach me how to lose my pulse, I will teach you how to find yours."

The man was happy. He knew he had come to the right place. Finally, he would find his pulse.

Both men were lying on the floor holding hands. All of a sudden they were lifted up and they were now lying on the clouds. They were flying around the world. The wise man was losing his pulse and the other man was gaining his.

When they landed on the floor, each one was happy. The man without a pulse didn't realize what was going to happen to him; neither did the wise man. The wise man became young and handsome and he learned to relax and not to worry. He knew that he lost his pulse and was now able to reach *Utopia*. The man without the pulse became old, worried and painful. He had found his pulse, heart and blood but lost his youth, vigor and strength.

You've wondered what this story was to do with me? Probably you will ask me if this is an the allegory about my life. Losing a loved one, and surviving is one of the hardest things in life. At first you're numb, then you're alive again. At first you cry, then you grieve.

Life's lesson is that we cannot merely achieve material ends, but that we must strive for the human virtues necessary to live and love happily together. We live in the hearts of friends; loved ones who have passed before us. The moral of the story: be happy with what you've got because pretty quick you may have nothing.

I took my wife for granted, and now that she has gone I miss her.

Epilogue

Before my wife died she wrote three letters that we have kept. These letters helped us after her death and still keep us alive.

"Dear Benjamin: I love you very much. The day that you were born was the happiest day in my life. I knew you were stubborn and had your own mind. You were determined to have a career, and I hope that very soon you will find a mate to fill your life with happiness.

Your success didn't come easy. You studied and worked very hard. Please know that your success made me very proud of you. Take good care of your father which I am sure you will do and take good care of your sister.

Your loving mother."

"Dear Sophia: When you get this letter I will already be gone. I love you very much, Sophia. Our relationship was very strange. It was a love and hate relationship. I hated and loved my mother and my mother had the same relationship with her mother. My mother never supported me in any major life decision, school, marriage, my family. Sophia now you are married. I hope that very soon you will have children. If one of them is a girl please break the cycle of hate and love.

You must be more sensitive to your daughter than I was to you and my mother was to me. Always remember that your words are love to your children and choose them carefully. Eat them when they will cause pain, say them when they are filled with love.

Please take good care of your father and your brother and yourself. If you take good care of yourself then you will be able to take good care of the rest of the world.

Your loving mother."

"Dear Alex, Alexander or Alejandro: I don't know what to call you, but every name I called you was a loving name. I lived with you for 32 years. I lived with you longer than I lived with my parents. Just like my first word was "Mamie." My last words will be "Alex, I love you very much." Alex, I had a good life. I chose the moment to be born and I will choose the moment to die.

Don't be foolish. Get married and enjoy life. Once you are happy I am going to be happy and once you are sad, I am sad. Remember, once you are kissing your new wife it is as if you are kissing me. Take good care of yourself and the children. The children will take good care of you.

I had a wonderful life with you. I am 53 years old and I am ready to die. I am taking the easy road leaving you but you are taking the hard one. When you are sad and unhappy remember the good times. Being together the first few years of our marriage, holding hands, eating together and thinking only about ourselves. Remember the birth of our children, watching them in the delivery room, holding their hands and cutting the umbilical cord. Taking our children to school. Planning our daily routine and saving our money for vacations and higher education for our children.

It is so funny that I always worried about you, Alex, and the kids. I thought I would live forever and now I am dying.

Love, your Margaret."

>-+-4>-0-<+-+-<

These letters comfort my children and me. Only time was able to heal us, and life continues.

I hope you enjoyed reading this book as much as I enjoyed writing it.

Class Critics

Here are some of the critiques of my book written by my high school students.

"Mr. Modena succeeds in arousing our sympathy and understanding of his great loss of his wife.
He also opens our eyes to the life that people live in a convalescent home."

"Love comes in many faces. Mr. Modena, you wrote your book with so much love. Why did you title it People Without Faces? I love the book but love has many beautiful faces, not forgotten ones."

"I didn't like the book too much, especially the story about friendship. The story is an illusion and what we want friendship to be and not what it really is. People very usually like to write fantasies, because you only see what you want to see and Mr. Modena wrote what he saw and not what was really there."

"Mr. Modena, your book from what you read us was beautiful. It was deep. I could tell you put your heart into this book. I got in trouble at home at supper time; instead of eating with the family I read your book. I usually hate to read."

"I thought the book was very good and detailed. I liked that it had a lot of voices and emotion. It almost made me cry. I don't cry, I play football for my school."

"If I give you a good critique, do I get extra credit? If I don't critique the book, are we even? And if I give you a bad critique, will you punish me? So far the book is ok."

"Dear Mr. Modena: I know you are old and retired and need a hobby. Why don't you let real authors write books and for a hobby, collect butterflies?"

"The book was very meaningful and had a good lesson to be heard."

"Mr. Modena, I think it is very great that you are writing about your past, because it really touches another person. There are many lessons learned. I am glad that you have shared them with us. The stories about your kids were very touching."